Concurrency by Tutorials

By Scott Grosch

Concurrency by Tutorials

By Scott Grosch

Notice of Rights

Notice of Liability

Trademarks

ISBN: 978-1-950325-91-7

Table of Contents

Book License

By purchasing *Concurrency by Tutorials*, you have the following license:

- You are allowed to use and/or modify the source code in *Concurrency by Tutorials* in as many apps as you want, with no attribution required.
- You are allowed to use and/or modify all art, images and designs that are included in *Concurrency by Tutorials* in as many apps as you want, but must include this attribution line somewhere inside your app: "Artwork/images/designs: from *Concurrency by Tutorials*, available at www.kodeco.com".
- The source code included in *Concurrency by Tutorials* is for your personal use only. You are NOT allowed to distribute or sell the source code in *Concurrency by Tutorials* without prior authorization.
- This book is for your personal use only. You are NOT allowed to reproduce or transmit any part of this book by any means, electronic or mechanical, including photocopying, recording, etc. without previous authorization. You may not sell digital versions of this book or distribute them to friends, coworkers or students without prior authorization. They need to purchase their own copies.

All materials provided with this book are provided on an "as is" basis, without warranty of any kind, express or implied, including but not limited to the warranties of merchantability, fitness for a particular purpose and noninfringement. In no event shall the authors or copyright holders be liable for any claim, damages or other liability, whether in an action or contract, tort or otherwise, arising from, out of or in connection with the software or the use or other dealings in the software.

All trademarks and registered trademarks appearing in this guide are the properties of their respective owners.

Before You Begin

This section tells you a few things you need to know before you get started, such as what you'll need for hardware and software, where to find the project files for this book and more.

What You Need

To follow along with this book, you'll need the following:

- A Mac running **macOS Ventura** (13.0) or later. Earlier versions might work, but they're untested.
- **Xcode 14 or later**. Xcode is the main development tool for iOS. While earlier versions of Xcode should work, the examples in this book have been specifically tested on Xcode 14 and iOS 16. You can download the latest version of Xcode from Apple's developer site here: apple.co/2asi58y
- **An intermediate level knowledge of Swift**. This book teaches concurrency when building iOS applications using Swift. You could use the knowledge acquired in this book for your Objective-C codebase, but this book won't include any Objective-C examples. You could also use this knowledge for your macOS, tvOS and watchOS apps, but like Objective-C, this book won't include any examples for these platforms.

If you want to try things out on a physical iOS device, you'll need a developer account with Apple, which you can obtain for free. However, all the sample projects in this book will work just fine in the iOS Simulator bundled with Xcode, so the paid developer account is completely optional.

Book Source Code & Forums

Where to Download the Materials for This Book

The materials for this book can be cloned or downloaded from the GitHub book materials repository:

- https://github.com/kodecocodes/con-materials/tree/editions/3.0

Forums

We've also set up an official forum for the book at https://forums.kodeco.com/c/books/concurrency-by-tutorials. This is a great place to ask questions about the book or to submit any errors you may find.

"This book is dedicated to my wife and daughter, as well as to my parents who always made sure a good education was a priority."

— *Scott Grosch*

About the Author

Scott Grosch is the author of this book. He has been involved with iOS app development since the first release of the public SDK from Apple. He mostly works with a small set of clients on a couple large apps. During the day, Scott is a Solutions Architect at a Fortune 500 company in the Pacific Northwest. At night, he's still working on figuring out how to be a good parent to a toddler with his wife.

About the Editor

Marin Bencevic is a computer vision researcher working on medical images. His other passion is iOS development, and he enjoys working on cool iOS apps and games, nerding out about programming languages, learning new things and then blogging about them. He also has a chubby cat.

Acknowledgments

We'd like to thank:

Luke Freeman & **Adriana Kutenko** for coordinating and/or creating many of the images that you see in this book.

Amy Sawatzky for her editorial assistance to the author.

Section I: Getting Started With Concurrency

In this part of the book, you're going to learn about the basics of Concurrency. You're going to learn what it is, what kind of problems it solves and when and how you would use it.

Furthermore, you will learn the basic pieces which comprise Concurrency in iOS development: **Grand Central Dispatch** and **Operations**.

This section will provide you with foundational knowledge regarding Concurrency, so be sure to read it through! The upcoming sections will dive much deeper into each of these concepts individually.

Chapter 1: Introduction

Performance. Responsiveness. They're not glamorous tasks. When done properly, nobody is going to thank you. When done incorrectly, app retention is going to suffer and you'll be dinged during your next yearly performance review.

There are a multitude of ways in which an app can be optimized for speed, performance and overall responsiveness. This book will focus on the topic of **concurrency**.

What Is Concurrency?

Wikipedia defines concurrency as "the decomposability property of a program, algorithm, or problem into order-independent or partially-ordered components or units." What this means is looking at the logic of your app to determine which pieces can run at the same time, and possibly in a random order, yet still result in a correct implementation of your data flow.

Moderns devices almost always have more than a single CPU, and Apple's iPhones have been dual core since 2011. Having more than one core means they are capable of running more than a single task at the same time. By splitting your app into logical "chunks" of code you enable the iOS device to run multiple parts of your program at the same time, thus improving overall performance.

Why Use Concurrency?

It's critical to ensure that your app runs as smoothly as possible and that the end user is not ever forced to wait for something to happen. A second is a minuscule amount of time for most everything not related to a computer. However, if a human has to wait a second to see a response after taking an action on a device like an iPhone, it feels like an eternity. "It's too slow" is one of the main contributors to your app being uninstalled.

Scrolling through a table of images is one of the more common situations wherein the end user will be impacted by the lack of concurrency. If you need to download an image from the network, or perform some type of image processing before displaying it, the scrolling will stutter and you'll be forced to display multiple "busy" indicators instead of the expected image.

A beneficial side effect to using concurrency is that it helps you to spend a bit more time thinking about your app's overall architecture. Instead of just writing massive methods to "get the job done" you'll find yourself naturally writing smaller, more manageable methods that can run concurrently.

How to Use Concurrency

That's the focus of this book! At a high level you need to structure your app so that some tasks can run at the same time. Multiple tasks that modify the same resource (i.e., variable) can't run at the same time, unless you make them thread safe.

Tasks which access different resources, or *read-only* shared resources, can all be accessed via different threads to allow for much faster processing.

This book will focus on the two main ways that iOS provides you with the ability to run code concurrently. The first section on **Grand Central Dispatch** will cover the common scenarios where you will find yourself being able to implement concurrency. You'll learn how to run tasks in the background, how to group tasks together and how to handle restricting the number of tasks that can run at once. By the end of the first section you'll also have a strong grasp of the dangers of concurrency and how to avoid them.

In the second section you'll focus on the `Operation` class. Built on top of Grand Central Dispatch, operations allow for the handling of more complex scenarios such as reusable code to be run on a background thread, having one thread depend on another, and even canceling an operation before it's started or completed.

Most modern programming languages provide for some form of concurrency and Swift is of course no exception. Different languages use widely different mechanisms for handling concurrency. C# and Typescript, for example use an *async/await* pattern, whereas Swift uses closures to handle what runs on another thread. Swift 5 originally had plans to implement the more common *async/await* pattern but it was removed from the specification until the next release.

Where to Go From Here?

Well to the next page of course! Hopefully as you work through the following chapters you'll gain an appreciation for what concurrency can do for your app and why your end users will appreciate the extra effort you put into making the app perform as fast as possible. Knowing when to use Grand Central Dispatch as opposed to an `Operation` subclass early in the app lifecycle will save you hours of rework down the road.

Chapter 2: GCD vs. Operations

There are two APIs that you'll use when making your app concurrent: **Grand Central Dispatch**, commonly referred to as **GCD**, and **Operations**. These are neither competing technologies nor something that you have to exclusively pick between. In fact, Operations are built on top of GCD!

Grand Central Dispatch

GCD is Apple's implementation of C's **libdispatch** library. Its purpose is to queue up **tasks** — either a method or a closure — that can be run in parallel, depending on availability of resources; it then executes the tasks on an available processor core.

> **Note**: Apple's documentation sometimes refers to a **block** in lieu of **closure**, since that was the name used in Objective-C. You can consider them interchangeable in the context of concurrency.

While GCD uses threads in its implementation, you, as the developer, do not need to worry about managing them yourself. GCD's tasks are so lightweight to enqueue that Apple, in its 2009 technical brief on GCD, stated that only 15 instructions are required for implementation, whereas creating traditional threads could require several hundred instructions.

All of the tasks that GCD manages for you are placed into GCD-managed **first-in, first-out** (FIFO) queues. Each task that you submit to a queue is then executed against a pool of threads fully managed by the system.

> **Note**: There is no guarantee as to which thread your task will execute against.

Synchronous and Asynchronous Tasks

Work placed into the queue may either run **synchronously** or **asynchronously**. When running a task synchronously, your app will wait and block the current run loop until execution finishes before moving on to the next task. Alternatively, a task that is run asynchronously will start, but return execution to your app immediately. This way, the app is free to run other tasks while the first one is executing.

> **Note**: It's important to keep in mind that, while the queues are FIFO based, that does not ensure that tasks will finish in the order you submit them. The FIFO procedure applies to when the task *starts*, not when it finishes.

In general, you'll want to take any long-running non-UI task that you can find and make it run asynchronously in the background. GCD makes this very simple via closures with a few lines of code, like so:

```
// Class level variable
let queue = DispatchQueue(label: "com.yourcompany.worker")

// Somewhere in your function
queue.async {
  // Call slow non-UI methods here

  DispatchQueue.main.async {
    // Update the UI here
  }
}
```

You'll learn all about `DispatchQueue` in Chapter 3, "Queues & Threads." In general, you create a queue, submit a task to it to run asynchronously on a background thread, and, when it's complete, you delegate the code back to the main thread to update the UI.

Serial and Concurrent Queues

The queue to which your task is submitted also has a characteristic of being either **serial** or **concurrent**. Serial queues only have a single thread associated with them and thus only allow a single task to be executed at any given time. A concurrent queue, on the other hand, is able to utilize as many threads as the system has resources for. Threads will be created and released as necessary on a concurrent queue.

> **Note**: While you can tell iOS that you'd like to use a concurrent queue, remember that there is no *guarantee* that more than one task will run at a time. If your iOS device is completely bogged down and your app is competing for resources, it may only be capable of running a single task.

Asynchronous Doesn't Mean Concurrent

While the difference seems subtle at first, just because your tasks are *asynchronous* doesn't mean they will run *concurrently*. You're actually able to submit asynchronous tasks to either a serial queue or a concurrent queue. Being synchronous or asynchronous simply identifies whether or not the queue on which you're running the task must wait for the task to complete before it can spawn the next task.

On the other hand, categorizing something as *serial versus concurrent* identifies whether the queue has a *single* thread or *multiple* threads available to it. If you think about it, submitting three asynchronous tasks to a serial queue means that each task has to completely finish before the next task is able to start as there is only one thread available.

In other words, a task being synchronous or not speaks to the *source* of the task. Being serial or concurrent speaks to the *destination* of the task.

Operations

GCD is great for common tasks that need to be run a single time in the background. When you find yourself building functionality that should be reusable — such as image editing operations — you will likely want to encapsulate that functionality into a class. By subclassing `Operation`, you can accomplish that goal!

Operation Subclassing

`Operations` are fully-functional classes that can be submitted to an `OperationQueue`, just like you'd submit a closure of work to a `DispatchQueue` for GCD. Because they're classes and can contain variables, you gain the ability to know what state the operation is in at any given point.

Operations can exist in any of the following states:

- `isReady`
- `isExecuting`
- `isCancelled`
- `isFinished`

Unlike GCD, an operation is run synchronously by default, and getting it to run asynchronously requires more work. While you can directly execute an operation yourself, that's almost never going to be a good idea due to its synchronous nature. You'll want to get it off of the main thread by submitting it to an `OperationQueue` so that your UI performance isn't impacted.

Bonus Features

But wait, there's more! Operations provide greater control over your tasks as you can now handle such common needs as cancelling the task, reporting the state of the task, wrapping asynchronous tasks into an operation and specifying dependences between various tasks. Chapter 6, "Operations," will provide a more in-depth discussion of using operations in your app.

BlockOperation

Sometimes, you find yourself working on an app that heavily uses operations, but find that you have a need for a simpler, GCD-like, closure. If you don't want to also create a `DispatchQueue`, then you can instead utilize the `BlockOperation` class.

`BlockOperation` subclasses `Operation` for you and manages the concurrent execution of one or more closures on the default global queue. However, being an actual `Operation` subclass lets you take advantage of all the other features of an operation.

> **Note**: Block operations run concurrently. If you need them to run serially, you'll need to setup a dispatch queue instead.

Which Should You Use?

There's no clear-cut directive as to whether you should use GCD or Operations in your app. GCD tends to be simpler to work with for simple tasks you just need to execute and forget. Operations provide much more functionality when you need to keep track of a job or maintain the ability to cancel it.

If you're just working with methods or chunks of code that need to be executed, GCD is a fitting choice. If you're working with objects that need to encapsulate data and functionality then you're more likely to utilize Operations. Some developers even go to the extreme of saying that you should always use Operations because it's built on top of GCD, and Apple's guidance says to always use the highest level of abstraction provided.

At the end of the day, you should use whichever technology makes the most sense at the time and provides for the greatest long-term sustainability of your project, or specific use-case.

In the next chapter, you'll take a deep dive into how Grand Central Dispatch works, learn about the difference between threads and queues, and identify some of the complexities that can occur when implementing concurrency in your app.

Where to Go From Here?

To the next chapter, of course! The rest of the book will examine, in detail, both Grand Central Dispatch and Operations. By the time you've completed the book you'll have a solid grasp on what both options provide, as well as a better idea on how to choose one over the other.

Section II: Grand Central Dispatch

In this section, you'll take a deep dive into Apple's most popular and easy-to-use mechanism to write and manage concurrent tasks — Grand Central Dispatch. You'll learn how to utilize queues and threads to control the execution of tasks in your app, as well as how to group these tasks together. You'll also learn about common pitfalls and dangers of using concurrency, and how you can avoid them.

Chapter 3: Queues & Threads

Dispatch queues and threads have been mentioned a couple of times now, and you're probably wondering what they are at this point. In this chapter, you'll get a much deeper understanding of what Dispatch queue and Threads are, and how to best incorporate them in your development workflow.

Threads

You've probably heard the term **multithreading** at some point, yes? A **thread** is really short for **thread of execution**, and it's how a running **process** splits tasks across resources on the system. Your iOS app is a process that runs multiple tasks by utilizing multiple threads. You can have as many threads executing at once as you have cores in your device's CPU.

There are many advantages to splitting your app's work into multiple threads:

- **Faster execution**: By running tasks on threads, it's possible for work to be done *concurrently*, which will allow it to finish faster than running everything serially.
- **Responsiveness**: If you only perform user-visible work on the main UI thread, then users won't notice that the app slows down or freezes up periodically due to work that could be performed on another thread.
- **Optimized resource consumption**: Threads are highly optimized by the OS.

Sounds great, right? More cores, more threads, faster app. I bet you're ready to learn how to create one, right? Too bad! In reality, you should never find yourself needing to create a thread explicitly. The OS will handle all thread creation for you using higher abstractions.

Apple provides the APIs necessary for thread management, but if you try to directly manage them yourself, you could in fact degrade, rather than improve, performance. The OS keeps track of many statistics to know when it should and should not allocate or destroy threads. Don't fool yourself into thinking it's as simple as spinning up a thread when you want one. For those reasons, this book will not cover direct thread management.

Dispatch Queues

The way you work with threads is by creating a `DispatchQueue`. When you create a queue, the OS will potentially create and assign one or more threads to the queue. If existing threads are available, they can be reused; if not, then the OS will create them as necessary.

Creating a dispatch queue is pretty simple on your part, as you can see in the example below:

```
let label = "com.yourcompany.mycoolapp.networking"
let queue = DispatchQueue(label: label)
```

Phew, fairly easy, eh? Normally, you'd put the text of the label directly inside the initializer, but it's broken into separate statements for the sake of brevity.

The `label` argument simply needs to be any unique value for identification purposes. While you *could* simply use a UUID to guarantee uniqueness, it's best to use a reverse-DNS style name, as shown above (e.g. `com.company.app`), since the label is what you'll see when debugging and it's helpful to assign it meaningful text.

The Main Queue

When your app starts, a `main` dispatch queue is automatically created for you. It's a serial queue that's responsible for your UI. Because it's used so often, Apple has made it available as a class variable, which you access via `DispatchQueue.main`. You *never* want to execute something synchronously against the main queue, unless it's related to actual UI work. Otherwise, you'll lock up your UI which could potentially degrade your app performance.

If you recall from the previous chapter, there are two types of dispatch queues: *serial* or *concurrent*. The default initializer, as shown in the code above, will create a serial queue wherein each task must complete before the next task is able to start.

In order to create a concurrent queue, simply pass in the `.concurrent` attribute, like so:

```
let label = "com.yourcompany.mycoolapp.networking"
let queue = DispatchQueue(label: label, attributes: .concurrent)
```

Concurrent queues are so common that Apple has provided six different global concurrent queues, depending on the **Quality of service (QoS)** the queue should have.

Quality of Service

When using a concurrent dispatch queue, you'll need to tell iOS how important the tasks are that get sent to the queue so that it can properly prioritize the work that needs to be done against all the other tasks that are clamoring for resources. Remember that higher-priority work has to be performed faster, likely taking more system resources to complete and requiring more energy than lower-priority work.

If you just need a concurrent queue but don't want to manage your own, you can use the `global` class method on `DispatchQueue` to get one of the pre-defined global queues:

```
let queue = DispatchQueue.global(qos: .userInteractive)
```

As mentioned above, Apple offers six quality of service classes:

.userInteractive

The `.userInteractive` QoS is recommended for tasks that the user *directly interacts* with. UI-updating calculations, animations or anything needed to keep the UI responsive and fast. If the work doesn't happen quickly, things may appear to freeze. Tasks submitted to this queue should complete virtually instantaneously.

.userInitiated

The `.userInitiated` queue should be used when the *user* kicks off a task from the UI that needs to happen immediately, but can be done asynchronously. For example, you may need to open a document or read from a local database. If the user clicked a button, this is probably the queue you want. Tasks performed in this queue should take a few seconds or less to complete.

.utility

You'll want to use the `.utility` dispatch queue for tasks that would typically include a progress indicator such as long-running computations, I/O, networking or continuous data feeds. The system tries to balance responsiveness and performance with energy efficiency. Tasks can take a few seconds to a few minutes in this queue.

.background

For tasks that the user is not directly aware of you should use the `.background` queue. They don't require user interaction and aren't time sensitive. Prefetching, database maintenance, synchronizing remote servers and performing backups are all great examples. The OS will focus on energy efficiency instead of speed. You'll want to use this queue for work that will take significant time, on the order of minutes or more.

.default and .unspecified

There are two other possible choices that exist, but you should not use explicitly. There's a `.default` option, which falls between `.userInitiated` and `.utility` and is the default value of the `qos` argument. It's not intended for you to directly use. The second option is `.unspecified`, and exists to support legacy APIs that may opt the thread out of a quality of service. It's good to know they exist, but if you're using them, you're almost certainly doing something wrong.

> **Note**: Global queues are always concurrent and first-in, first-out.

Inferring QoS

If you create your own concurrent dispatch queue, you can tell the system what the QoS is via its initializer:

```
let queue = DispatchQueue(label: label,
                          qos: .userInitiated,
                          attributes: .concurrent)
```

However, this is like arguing with your spouse/kids/dogs/pet rock: Just because you say it doesn't make it so! The OS will pay attention to what type of tasks are being submitted to the queue and make changes as necessary.

If you submit a task with a higher quality of service than the queue has, the queue's level will increase. Not only that, but all the operations enqueued will also have their priority raised as well.

If the current context is the main thread, the inferred QoS is `.userInitiated`. You can specify a QoS yourself, but as soon as you'll add a task with a higher QoS, your queue's QoS service will be increased to match it.

Adding Task to Queues

Dispatch queues provide both `sync` and `async` methods to add a task to a queue. Remember that, by **task**, I simply mean, "*Whatever block of code you need to run.*" When your app starts, for example, you may need to contact your server to update the app's state. That's not user initiated, doesn't need to happen immediately and depends on networking I/O, so you should send it to the global utility queue:

```
DispatchQueue.global(qos: .utility).async {
  guard let self else { return }

  // Perform your work here
  // ...

  // Switch back to the main queue to
  // update your UI
  DispatchQueue.main.async {
    self.label = "New articles available!"
  }
}
```

There are two key points you should take away from the above code sample. First, there's nothing special about a `DispatchQueue` that nullifies the closure rules. You still need to make sure that you're properly handling the closure's captured variables, such as `self`, if you plan to utilize them.

Strongly capturing `self` in a GCD `async` closure will not cause a reference cycle (e.g. a retain cycle) since the whole closure will be deallocated once it's completed, but it *will* extend the lifetime of `self`. For instance, if you make a network request from a view controller that has been dismissed in the meantime, the closure will still get called. If you capture the view controller weakly, it will be `nil`. However, if you capture it strongly, the view controller will remain alive until the closure finishes its work. Keep that in mind and capture weakly or strongly based on your needs.

Second, notice how updates to the UI are dispatched to the `main` queue *inside* the dispatch to the background queue. It's not only OK, but very common, to nest `async` type calls inside others.

Note: You should *never* perform UI updates on any queue other than the main queue. If it's not documented what queue an API callback uses, dispatch it to the main queue!

Use extreme caution when submitting a task to a dispatch queue synchronously. If you find yourself calling the `sync` method, instead of the `async` method, think once or twice whether that's really what you should be doing. If you submit a task synchronously to the current queue, which blocks the current queue, and your task tries to access a resource in the current queue, then your app will **deadlock**, which is explained more in Chapter 5, "Concurrency Problems." Similarly, if you call `sync` from the `main` queue, you'll block the thread that updates the UI and your app will appear to freeze up.

> **Note**: Never call `sync` from the main thread, since it would block your main thread and could even potentially cause a deadlock.

Image Loading Example

You've been inundated with quite a bit of theoretical concepts at this point. Time to see an actual example!

In the downloadable materials for this book, you'll find a starter project for this chapter. Open up the **Concurrency.xcodeproj** project. Build and run the app. You'll see some images slowly load from the network into a `LazyVGrid`. If you try to scroll the screen while the images are loading, either nothing will happen or the scrolling will be very slow and choppy, depending on the speed of the device you are using.

Open up **ContentView** and take a look at what's going on. When the view loads, it just grabs a static list of image URLs to be displayed. In a production app, of course, you'd likely be making a network call at this point to generate a list of items to display, but for this example it's easier to hardcode a list of images.

Now look at the `download` method in **Cell**. That's where the trouble happens. You can see that when a cell is ready to be displayed a call is made via one of `Data`'s constructors to download the image and then it's assigned to the cell. The code looks simple enough, and it is what most starting iOS developers would do to download an image, but you saw the results: a choppy, underperforming UI experience!

Unless you slept through the previous pages of explanation, you know by now that the work to download the image, which is a network call, needs to be done on a separate thread from the UI.

> **Mini-challenge**: Which queue do you think should handle the image download? Take a look back a few pages and make your decision.

Did you pick either `.userInteractive` or `.userInitiated`? It's tempting to do because the end result is directly visible to the user but the reality is if you used that logic then you'd never use any other queue. The proper choice here is to use the `.utility` queue. You've got no control over how long a network call will take to complete and you want the OS to properly balance the speed vs. battery life of the device.

Using a Global Queue

Create a new method in `Cell` that starts off like so:

```
private func downloadWithGlobalQueue() {
  DispatchQueue.global(qos: .utility).async {
  }
}
```

You'll eventually call this from `body` to perform the actual image processing. Begin by copying the entire contents of the `download` method into the `async` call's block, then delete the `download` method. Fix the compiler error now by calling `downloadWithGlobalQueue` instead inside the `task` block of the `body`.

Even though it's a synchronous operation that's being performed, it is running on a separate thread and thus the UI isn't impacted. Remember that updates to the UI can only happen on the main thread! Wrap the `image` assignment inside of another dispatch:

```
DispatchQueue.main.async {
  image = Image(uiImage: uiImage)
}
```

Notice that the bare minimum of code is being sent back to the main thread. Do every bit of work that you can before dispatching to the main queue so that your UI remains as responsive as possible.

Build and run your app again. Once your app starts loading images, scroll the view. Notice how silky smooth that scrolling is! Of course, you might notice some issues: the images pop in and out of existence, load pretty slowly and keep being reloaded when you scroll away. You'll need a way to start and cancel these requests and cache their results to make the experience perfect. These are all things which are much easier using operations instead of Grand Central Dispatch, which you'll cover in later chapters. So keep reading! :]

Using Built-in Methods

You can see how simple the above changes were to vastly improve the performance of your app. However, it's not always necessary to grab a dispatch queue yourself. Many of the standard iOS libraries handle that for you. Add the following method:

```
private func downloadWithUrlSession() {
  URLSession.shared.dataTask(with: url) { data, _, _ in
    guard let data, let uiImage = UIImage(data: data) else {
      return
    }

    DispatchQueue.main.async {
      image = Image(uiImage: uiImage)
    }
  }
  .resume()
}
```

Notice how, this time, instead of getting a dispatch queue, you directly used the `dataTask` method on `URLSession`. The code is *almost* the same, but it handles the download of the data for you so that you don't have to do it yourself, nor do you need to grab a dispatch queue. Always prefer to use the system provided methods when they are available as it will make your code not only more future-proof but easier to read for other developers. A junior programmer might not understand what the dispatch queues are, but they understand making a network call.

If you call `downloadWithUrlSession` instead of `downloadWithGlobalQueue` in `body` you should see the exact same result after building and running your app again.

Using DispatchWorkItem

There's another way to submit work to a `DispatchQueue` besides passing an anonymous closure. `DispatchWorkItem` is a class that provides an actual object to hold the code you wish to submit to a queue.

For example, the following code:

```
let queue = DispatchQueue(label: "xyz")
queue.async {
  print("The block of code ran!")
}
```

Would work exactly like this piece of code:

```
let queue = DispatchQueue(label: "xyz")
let workItem = DispatchWorkItem {
  print("The block of code ran!")
}
queue.async(execute: workItem)
```

Canceling a Work Item

One reason you might wish to use an explicit `DispatchWorkItem` is if you have a need to cancel the task before, or during, execution. If you call `cancel()` on the work item one of two actions will be performed:

1. If the task has not yet started on the queue, it will be removed.

2. If the task is currently executing, the `isCancelled` property will be set to `true`.

You'll need to check the `isCancelled` property periodically in your code and take appropriate action to cancel the task, if possible.

Poor Man's Dependencies

The `DispatchWorkItem` class also provides a `notify(queue:execute:)` method which can be used to identify another `DispatchWorkItem` that should be executed after the current work item completes.

```
let queue = DispatchQueue(label: "xyz")
let backgroundWorkItem = DispatchWorkItem { }
let updateUIWorkItem = DispatchWorkItem { }

backgroundWorkItem.notify(queue: DispatchQueue.main,
                          execute: updateUIWorkItem)
queue.async(execute: backgroundWorkItem)
```

Notice that when specifying a follow-on work item to be executed, you must explicitly specify which queue the work item should execute against.

If you find yourself needing the ability to cancel a task or specify dependencies, I strongly suggest you instead refer to Chapter 9, "Operation Dependencies" and Chapter 10, "Canceling Operations" in Section III, "Operations."

Where to Go From Here?

At this point, you should have a good grasp of what dispatch queues are, what they're used for and how to use them. Play around with the code samples from above to ensure you understand how they work.

The sample app is of course somewhat contrived so as to easily showcase how a `DispatchQueue` works. There are many other performance improvements that could be made to the sample app but those will have to wait for Chapter 7, "Operation Queues."

Now that you've seen the benefits, the next chapter will introduce you to the dangers of implementing concurrency in your app.

Chapter 4: Groups & Semaphores

Sometimes, instead of just tossing a job into a queue, you need to process a group of jobs. They don't all have to run at the same time, but you need to know when they have all completed. Apple provides **Dispatch Groups** for this exact scenario.

DispatchGroup

The aptly named `DispatchGroup` class is what you'll use when you want to track the completion of a *group* of tasks.

You start by initializing a `DispatchGroup`. Once you have one and want to track a task as part of that group, you can provide the group as an argument to the `async` method on any dispatch queue:

```
let group = DispatchGroup()

someQueue.async(group: group) { ... your work ... }
someQueue.async(group: group) { ... more work .... }
someOtherQueue.async(group: group) { ... other work ... }

group.notify(queue: DispatchQueue.main) {
  label = "All jobs have completed"
}
```

As seen in the example code above, groups are not hardwired to a single dispatch queue. You can use a single group, yet submit jobs to multiple queues, depending on the priority of the task that needs to be run. `DispatchGroup`s provide a `notify(queue:)` method, which you can use to be notified as soon as every job submitted has finished.

> **Note**: The notification is itself asynchronous, so it's possible to submit more jobs to the group after calling notify, as long as the previously submitted jobs have not already completed.

You'll notice that the `notify` method takes a dispatch queue as a parameter. When the jobs are all finished, the closure that you provide will be executed in the indicated dispatch queue. The `notify` call shown is likely to be the version you'll use most often, but there are a couple other versions which allow you to specify a quality of service as well, for example.

Synchronous Waiting

There be dragons here!

If, for some reason, you can't respond asynchronously to the group's completion notification, then you can instead use the `wait` method on the dispatch group. This is a *synchronous* method that will block the current queue until all the jobs have finished. It takes an optional parameter which specifies how long to wait for the tasks to complete. If not specified, then there is an infinite wait time:

```
let group = DispatchGroup()

someQueue.async(group: group) { ... }
someQueue.async(group: group) { ... }
someOtherQueue.async(group: group) { ... }

if group.wait(timeout: .now() + 60) == .timedOut {
  print("The jobs didn't finish in 60 seconds")
}
```

> **Note**: Remember, this *blocks* the current thread; never **ever** call `wait` on the main queue.

In the above example, you're giving the tasks up to 60 seconds to complete their work before `wait` returns.

It's important to know that the jobs *will* still run, even after the timeout has happened. To see this in practice, go to the starter projects in this chapter's download materials and open the playground named **DispatchGroup.playground**.

In the playground, the code adds two jobs to a dispatch group: one that takes 10 seconds (job 1) and another one that takes two seconds to complete:

```
let group = DispatchGroup()
let queue = DispatchQueue.global(qos: .userInitiated)

queue.async(group: group) {
    print("Start job 1")
    Thread.sleep(until: .now + 10)
    print("End job 1")
}

queue.async(group: group) {
    print("Start job 2")
    Thread.sleep(until: .now + 2)
```

```
    print("End job 2")
}
```

It then synchronously waits for the group to complete:

```
if group.wait(timeout: .now() + 5) == .timedOut {
  print("I got tired of waiting")
} else {
  print("All the jobs have completed")
}
```

Run the playground and look at the output on the right side of the Xcode window. You'll immediately see messages telling you that jobs 1 and 2 have started. After two seconds, you'll see a message saying job 2 has completed, and then three seconds later a message saying, "I got tired of waiting."

You can see from the sample that job 2 only sleeps for two seconds and that's why it can complete. You specified five total seconds of time to wait, and that's not enough for job 1 to complete, so the timeout message was printed.

However, if you wait another five seconds — you've already waited five and job 1 takes ten seconds — you'll see the completion message for job 1.

At this point, calling a synchronous wait method like this should be a **code smell** to you, potentially pointing out other issues in your architecture. Sure, it's much easier to implement synchronously, but the entire reason you're reading this book is to learn how to make your app perform as fast as possible. Having a thread just spin and continually ask, "Is it done yet?" isn't the best use of system resources.

Wrapping Asynchronous Methods

A dispatch queue natively knows how to work with dispatch groups, and it takes care of signaling to the system that a job has completed for you. In this case, **completed** means that the code block has run its course. Why does that matter? Because if you call an asynchronous method inside of your closure, then the closure will *complete* before the internal asynchronous method has completed.

You've got to somehow tell the task that it's not done until those internal calls have completed as well. In such a case, you can call the provided `enter` and `leave` methods on `DispatchGroup`.

Think of them like a simple count of running tasks. Every time you `enter`, the count goes up by 1. When you `leave`, the count goes down by 1:

```
queue.dispatch(group: group) {
  // count is 1
  group.enter()
  // count is 2
  someAsyncMethod {
    defer { group.leave() }

    // Perform your work here,
    // count goes back to 1 once complete
  }
}
```

By calling `group.enter()`, you let the dispatch group know that there's another block of code running, which should be counted towards the group's overall completion status. You, of course, have to pair that with a corresponding `group.leave()` call or you'll never be signaled of completion. Because you have to call `leave` even during error conditions, you will usually want to use a `defer` statement, as shown above, so that, no matter how you exit the closure, the `group.leave()` code executes.

In a simple case similar to the previous code sample, you can simply call the `enter` / `leave` pairs directly. If you're going to use `someAsyncMethod` frequently with dispatch groups, you should wrap the method to ensure you never forget to make the necessary calls:

```
func myAsyncAdd(
  lhs: Int,
  rhs: Int,
  completion: @escaping (Int) -> Void) {
  // Lots of cool code here
  completion(lhs + rhs)
}

func myAsyncAddForGroups(
  group: DispatchGroup,
  lhs: Int,
  rhs: Int,
  completion: @escaping (Int) -> Void) {
    group.enter()

    myAsyncAdd(first: first, second: second) { result in
      defer { group.leave() }
      completion(result)
    }
}
```

The wrapper method takes a parameter for the group that it will count against, and then the rest of the arguments should be exactly the same as that of the method you're wrapping. There's nothing special about wrapping the async method other than being 100% sure that the group `enter` and `leave` methods are properly handled.

If you write a wrapper method, then testing — you do test, right? — is simplified to a single location to validate proper pairing of `enter` and `leave` calls in all utilizations.

Downloading Images

Performing a network download should always be an asynchronous operation. This book's technical editor once had an assignment that required him to download all of the player's avatars before presenting the user with a list of players and their images. A dispatch group is a perfect solution for that task.

Please switch to the playground named **Images.playground** in this chapter's startup folder. Your task is to download each image from the provided `names` array in an asynchronous manner. When complete, you should show at least one of the images and terminate the playground. Take a moment to try and write the code yourself before continuing.

How'd you do? Clearly you're going to have to loop through the images to generate a URL, so start with that:

```
for id in ids {
  guard let url = URL(string: "\(base)\(id)-jpeg.jpg")
  else { continue }
```

Now that you've got a valid URL, call `URLSession`'s `dataTask` method. That's asynchronous already, so you'll need to handle the group's entry and exit:

```
group.enter()

let task = URLSession.shared.dataTask(with: url) {
  data, _, error in
```

As always, with asynchronous code, the `defer` statement is going to be your friend. Now that you've started the asynchronous task, regardless of how it exits, you've got to tell the dispatch group that the task has completed. If you don't, the app will hang forever waiting for completion:

```
defer { group.leave() }
```

After that, it's just a matter of converting the image and adding it to the array:

```
      if error == nil,
        let data = data,
        let image = UIImage(data: data) {
        images.append(image)
      }
    }

    task.resume()
  }
```

Due to properly handling the `enter` and `leave` pairs, you no longer have to spin and wait synchronously for the groups to enter. Use the `notify(queue:)` callback method to be informed when all image downloads have completed. Add this code outside the `for` loop:

```
group.notify(queue: queue) {
  images[0]

  PlaygroundPage.current.finishExecution()
}
```

If you run the playground now and watch the sidebar, you'll see each job starting, the images downloading, and eventually the notification triggering with the first image of the bunch.

Semaphores

There are times when you really need to control how many threads have access to a shared resource. You've already seen the read/write pattern to limit access to a single thread, but there are times when you can allow more resources to be used at once while still maintaining control over the total thread count.

If you're downloading data from the network, for example, you may wish to limit how many downloads happen at once.

You'll use a dispatch queue to offload the work, and you'll use dispatch groups so that you know when all the downloads have completed. However, you only want to allow four downloads to happen at once because you know the data you're getting is quite large and resource-heavy to process.

By using a DispatchSemaphore, you can handle exactly that use case. Before any desired use of the resource, you simply call the wait method, which is a synchronous function, and your thread will pause execution until the resource is available. If nothing has claimed ownership yet, you immediately get access. If somebody else has it, you'll wait until they signal that they're done with it.

When creating a **semaphore**, you specify how many concurrent accesses to the resource are allowed. If you wish to enable four network downloads at once, then you pass in 4. If you're trying to lock a resource for exclusive access, then you'd just specify 1.

Open up the playground named **Semaphores.playground** and you'll find some simple boilerplate code to set up the group and queue. After the line that assigns the dispatch queue, create a semaphore that allow four concurrent accesses:

```
let semaphore = DispatchSemaphore(value: 4)
```

You'll want to simulate performing 10 network downloads, so create a loop that dispatches onto the queue, using the group. Right after creating the semaphore, implement the loop:

```
for i in 1...10 {
  queue.async(group: group) {

  }
}
```

There shouldn't be anything surprising there as it's the same type of code you just saw. On each download thread, you now want to ask for permission to use the resource. To simulate the network download, you can just have the thread sleep for three seconds. Insert this code inside the async block:

```
semaphore.wait()
defer { semaphore.signal() }

print("Downloading image \(i)")

// Simulate a network wait
Thread.sleep(forTimeInterval: 3)

print("Downloaded image \(i)")
```

Just as you had to be sure to call `leave` on a dispatch group, you'll want to be sure to signal when you're done using the resource. Using a `defer` block is the best option as there's then no way to leave without letting go of the resource.

If you run the playground, you should immediately see that four **downloads** happen, then, three seconds later, another four occur. Finally, three seconds after that, the final two complete.

That's a useful example just to prove that the semaphores are doing their job of limiting access to the network. However, you need to actually download something!

Remove everything in the playground after the creation of the `semaphore` variable and then copy the code from the **Images.playground** starting with the `let base` statement, and paste it immediately after creating the semaphore. The resource you're trying to control is the network, so you can let the URL get created in the `for` loop but, before you enter the group, you'll need to wait for an available semaphore, so add in a semaphore call just before `group.enter()`:

```
semaphore.wait()
```

You need to use both elements because the semaphore controls access to the resource, and the dispatch group is how you are tracking completion. Modify the `defer` statement as well to handle the release of the semaphore:

```
defer {
  group.leave()
  semaphore.signal()
}
```

The order of the lines doesn't really matter; I just like to have the semaphore be the **outer** element that starts and ends the task. Update the `DispatchSemaphore` to have a value of 2 instead of 4 and then run the playground. You should see it work as before, albeit slower due to the limitation of just two downloads happening at once.

Think of the semaphore itself as being some type of resource. If you have three hammers and four saws available, you'd want to create two semaphores to represent them:

```
let hammer = DispatchSemaphore(value: 3)
let saw = DispatchSemaphore(value: 4)
```

Where to Go From Here?

Modify the various values in the playgrounds to be sure you understand how both groups and semaphores work.

Can you think of cases in your previous or current apps that might have benefited from either one? Don't be concerned if you can't think of a use case for semaphores. They're an advanced topic that very rarely comes up in daily programming, but it's good to know they exist when you need them.

Now that you've seen how great concurrency with GCD can be, it's time to talk about some of the negative aspects.

Chapter 5: Concurrency Problems

Unfortunately, for all the benefits provided by dispatch queues, they're not a panacea for all performance issues. There are three well-known problems that you can run into when implementing concurrency in your app if you're not careful:

- Race conditions
- Deadlock
- Priority inversion

Race Conditions

Threads that share the same process, which also includes your app itself, share the same address space. What this means is that each thread is trying to read and write to the same shared resource. If you aren't careful, you can run into **race conditions** in which multiple threads are trying to write to the same variable at the same time.

Consider the example where you have two threads executing, and they're both trying to update your object's `count` variable. Reads and writes are separate tasks that the computer cannot execute as a single operation. Computers work on **clock cycles** in which each tick of the clock allows a single operation to execute.

> **Note**: Do not confuse a computer's clock cycle with the clock on your watch. An iPhone 14 has a 3.23 GHz processor, meaning it can perform 3,230,000,000 clock cycles per second!

Thread 1 and thread 2 both want to update the count, and so you write some nice clean code like so:

```
count += 1
```

Seems pretty innocuous, right? Break that statement down into its component parts, add a bit of hand-waving, and what you end up with is something like this:

1. Load value of variable `count` into memory.
2. Increment value of `count` by one in memory.
3. Write newly updated `count` back to disk.

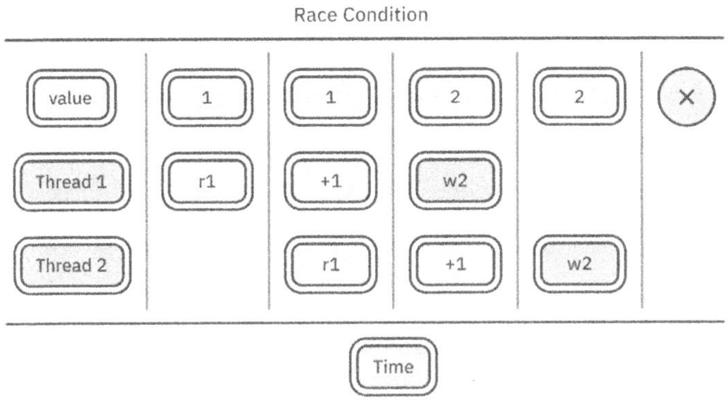

The graphic shows:

- Thread 1 kicked off a clock cycle before thread 2 and read the value 1 from `count`.
- On the second clock cycle, thread 1 updates the *in-memory* value to 2 and thread 2 reads the value 1 from `count`.
- On the third clock cycle, thread 1 now writes the value 2 back to the `count` variable. However, thread 2 is just now updating the *in-memory* value from 1 to 2.
- On the fourth clock cycle, thread 2 now also writes the value 2 to `count`... except you expected to see the value 3 because two separate threads both updated the value.

This type of race condition leads to incredibly complicated debugging due to the non-deterministic nature of these scenarios.

If thread 1 had started just two clock cycles earlier you'd have the value 3 as expected, but don't forget how many of these clock cycles happen per second.

You might run the program 20 times and get the correct result, then deploy it and start getting bug reports.

You can usually solve race conditions with a serial queue, as long as you know they are happening. If your program has a variable that needs to be accessed concurrently, you can wrap the reads and writes with a private queue, like this:

```
class ThreadableInt {
  private let queue = DispatchQueue(label: "...")
  private var _value = 0

  var value: Int {
    queue.sync { _value }
  }

  static func += (left: ThreadableInt, right: Int)  {
    left.increment(amount: right)
  }

  static func -= (left: ThreadableInt, right: Int)  {
    left.decrement(amount: right)
  }

  func increment(amount: Int = 1) -> Int {
    return queue.sync {
      _value += amount
      return _value
    }
  }
```

```
    func decrement(amount: Int = 1) -> Int {
      return queue.sync {
        _value -= amount
        return _value
      }
    }
  }
```

Notice how each access of `_value` is wrapped with a dispatch to the queue, preventing race conditions. You can verify both the issue and the solution by pasting the following into a playground:

```
var threadableInt = ThreadableInt()
DispatchQueue.concurrentPerform(iterations: 10_000) { _ in
    threadableInt += 1
}

print(threadableInt.value)

var dangerous = 1
DispatchQueue.concurrentPerform(iterations: 10_000) { _ in
    dangerous += 1
}

print(dangerous)
```

The playground will increment a variable 10,000 times concurrently, first using your new class, then using a simple integer. The `threadableInt` will always print the expected value 10,000, whereas the `dangerous` variable will normally print a value in the high 9k range.

Because you've not stated otherwise, the `queue` is a serial queue.

While you've created a usable solution, there are still many factors you need to keep in mind. The *way* you use the value is important. Consider this simple code:

```
if (threadableInt.value > 10 && threadableInt.value < 20) {
```

You've just introduced another possible failure. While each lookup is thread safe, you've used the value multiple times, meaning another thread might change the value in between the two comparisons. The solution will depend on your specific needs. Does it make sense to assign a temporary variable and compare against that? Do you need to add a method to `ThreadableInt` that allow you to pass a block of code which protects the entire thing via the `DispatchQueue`?

Just because you've wrapped your value, that doesn't solve every issue.

> **Note**: You can implement the same private queue sync for lazy variables, which might be run against multiple threads. If you don't, you could end up with two instances of the lazy variable initializer being run. Much like the variable assignment from before, the two threads could attempt to access the same lazy variable at nearly identical times. Once the second thread tries to access the lazy variable, it wasn't initialized *yet*, but it is about to be created by the access of the first thread. A classic race condition.

Dispatch Barrier

Sometimes, your shared resource requires more complex logic than a simple variable modification. You'll frequently see questions related to this online, and often they come with solutions related to locks and semaphores. Locking is very hard to implement properly. Instead, you can use Apple's **dispatch barrier** solution from GCD.

If you create a concurrent queue, you can process as many read type tasks as you want as they can all run at the same time.

When the variable needs to be written to, then you need to lock down the queue so that everything already submitted completes, but no new submissions are run until the update completes.

Usually you'll use a thread barrier when controlling access to an array. For example, consider a list of images, or an array of URLs. Looping through the array should not result in items changing during the iteration.

You implement a dispatch barrier approach this way:

```
class BarrierImages {
  // 1
  private let queue = DispatchQueue(label: "...",
attributes: .concurrent)

  private var _images: [Image] = []

  // 2
  var images: [Image] {
    var copied: [Image] = []

    queue.sync {
      copied = _images
    }
```

```
    return copied
  }

  func add(image: Image) {
    // 3
    queue.sync(flags: .barrier) { [weak self] in
      self?._images.append(image)
    }
  }

  func remove(at index: Int) -> Image? {
    var removed: Image? = nil

    // 4
    queue.sync(flags: .barrier) { [weak self] in
      removed = self?._images.remove(at: index)
    }

    return removed
  }
}
```

Here's what the above is doing:

1. When using dispatch barrier's you need to request a `concurrent` queue.
2. You'll need a method to return a copy of the array
3. Adding an item is a modification, so you'll need to add the `.barrier` flag.
4. Removing is also a modification, so provide the `.barrier` flag here as well.

Notice how you're now specifying that you want a concurrent queue and that the writes should be implemented with a barrier. The barrier task won't occur until all of the previous reads have completed.

Once the barrier hits, the queue pretends that it's serial and only the barrier task can run until completion. Once it completes, all tasks that were submitted after the barrier task can again run concurrently.

Deadlock

Imagine you're driving down a two-lane road on a bright sunny day and you arrive at your destination. Your destination is on the other side of the road, so you turn on the car's turn signal. You wait as tons of traffic drives in the other direction.

While waiting, five cars line up behind you. You then notice a car coming the other way with its turn signal on and it also stops a few cars past you, but it is now blocked by your backup.

Unfortunately, there are more cars behind the oncoming car and so the other lane backs up as well, blocking your ability to turn into your destination and clear the lane.

You've now reached **deadlock**, as you are both waiting on another task that can never complete. Neither of you can turn as cars are blocking the entrances to your destinations.

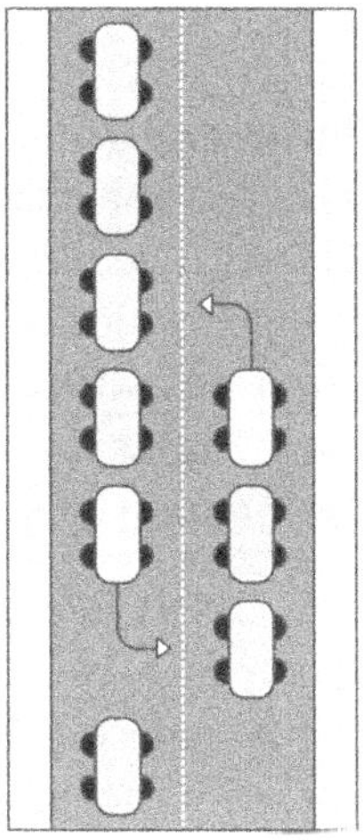

Deadlock is a pretty rare occurrence in Swift programming, unless you are using something like semaphores or other explicit locking mechanisms. Accidentally calling `sync` against the current dispatch queue is the most common occurrence of this that you'll run into.

If you're using semaphores to control access to multiple resources, be sure that you ask for resources in the same order. If thread 1 requests a hammer and then a saw, whereas thread 2 requests a saw and a hammer, you can deadlock. Thread 1 requests and receives a hammer at the same time thread 2 requests and receives a saw. Then thread 1 asks for a saw — without releasing the hammer — but thread 2 owns the resource so thread 1 must wait. Thread 2 asks for a saw, but thread 1 still owns the resource, so thread 2 must wait for the saw to become available. Both threads are now in deadlock as neither can progress until their requested resources are freed, which will never happen.

Priority Inversion

Technically speaking, **priority inversion** occurs when a queue with a lower quality of service is given higher **system priority** than a queue with a higher **quality of service**, or **QoS**. If you've been playing around with submitting tasks to queues, you've probably noticed a constructor to `async`, which takes a `qos` parameter.

Back in Chapter 3, "Queues & Threads," it was mentioned that the QoS of a queue is able to change, based on the work submitted to it. Normally, when you submit work to a queue, it takes on the priority of the queue itself. If you find the need to, however, you can specify that a specific task should have higher or lower priority than normal.

If you're using a `.userInitiated` queue and a `.utility` queue, and you submit multiple tasks to the latter queue with a `.userInteractive` quality of service (having a higher priority than `.userInitiated`), you could end up in the situation in which the latter queue is assigned a higher priority by the operating system. Suddenly all the tasks in the queue, most of which are really of the `.utility` quality of service, will end up running *before* the tasks from the `.userInitiated` queue. This is simple to avoid: If you need a higher quality of service, use a different queue!

The more common situation wherein priority inversion occurs is when a higher quality of service queue shares a resource with a lower quality of service queue. When the lower queue gets a lock on the object, the higher queue now has to wait. Until the lock is released, the high-priority queue is effectively *stuck* doing nothing while low-priority tasks run.

To see priority inversion in practice, open up the playground called **PriorityInversion.playground** from the **starter** project folder in this chapter's project materials.

In the code, you'll see three threads with different QoS values, as well as a semaphore:

```
let high = DispatchQueue.global(qos: .userInteractive)
let medium = DispatchQueue.global(qos: .userInitiated)
let low = DispatchQueue.global(qos: .background)

let semaphore = DispatchSemaphore(value: 1)
```

Then, various tasks are started on all queues:

```
high.async {
    // Wait 2 seconds just to be sure all the other tasks have
enqueued
    Thread.sleep(forTimeInterval: 2)
    semaphore.wait()
    defer { semaphore.signal() }

    print("High priority task is now running")
}

for i in 1...10 {
    medium.async {
        let waitTime = Double(exactly: arc4random_uniform(7))!
        print("Running medium task \(i)")
        Thread.sleep(forTimeInterval: waitTime)
    }
}

low.async {
    semaphore.wait()
    defer { semaphore.signal() }

    print("Running long, lowest priority task")
    Thread.sleep(forTimeInterval: 5)
}
```

If you display the console (Shift-Command-Y) and then run the playground, you'll see a different order each time you run:

```
Running medium task 7
Running medium task 6
Running medium task 1
Running medium task 4
Running medium task 2
Running medium task 8
Running medium task 5
Running medium task 3
Running medium task 9
Running medium task 10
Running long, lowest priority task
High priority task is now running
```

The end result is always the same. The high-priority task is always run *after* the medium and low-priority tasks due to priority inversion.

Where to Go From Here?

Throughout this chapter, you explored some common ways in which concurrent code can go wrong. While deadlock and priority inversion are much less common on iOS than other platforms, race conditions are definitely a concern you should be ready for.

If you're still eager to learn more about these common concurrency issues, the internet is full of excellent and surprising examples. In Chapter 12, "Thread Sanitizer," you'll lean more about how to track down race conditions in threading issues.

Section III: Operations

Even though Grand Central Dispatch provides most of the concurrency capabilties you'll need right out-of-the-box, sometimes you'll want some extra customizability. This is where Operations come into play. This section will teach you about Operations, Operation Queues and everything in between.

Chapter 6: Operations

Now that you're a ninja master of Grand Central Dispatch, it's time to shift gears and take a look at **operations**. In some regards, operations act very much like GCD, and it can be confusing as to the difference when you first start utilizing concurrency.

Both GCD and operations allow you to submit a chunk of code that should be run on a separate thread; however, operations allow for greater control over the submitted task.

As mentioned at the start of the book, operations are built on top of GCD. They add extra features such as dependencies on other operations, the ability to cancel the running operation, and an object-oriented model to support more complex requirements.

Reusability

One of the first reasons you'll likely want to create an `Operation` is for reusability. If you've got a simple "fire and forget" task, then GCD is likely all you'll need.

An `Operation` is an actual Swift object, meaning you can pass inputs to set up the task, implement helper methods, etc. Thus, you can wrap up a unit of work, or task, and execute it sometime in the future, and then easily submit that unit of work more than once.

Operation States

An operation has a state machine that represents its lifecycle. There are several possible states that occur at various parts of this lifecycle:

- When it's been instantiated and is ready to run, it will transition to the `isReady` state.
- At some point, you may invoke the `start` method, at which point it will move to the `isExecuting` state.
- If the app calls the `cancel` method, then it will transition to the `isCancelled` state before moving onto the `isFinished` state.
- If it's not canceled, then it will move directly from `isExecuting` to `isFinished`.

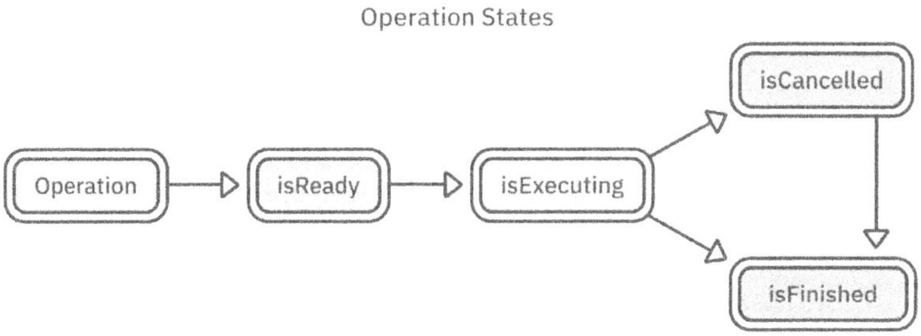

Each of the aforementioned states are read-only Boolean properties on the `Operation` class. You can query them at any point during the execution of the task to see whether or not the task is executing.

The `Operation` class handles all of these state transitions for you. The only two you can directly influence are the `isExecuting` state, by starting the operation, and the `isCancelled` state, if you call the `cancel` method on the object.

BlockOperation

You can quickly create an `Operation` out of a block of code using the `BlockOperation` class. Normally, you would simply pass a closure to its initializer:

```
let operation = BlockOperation {
  print("2 + 3 = \(2 + 3)")
}
```

A `BlockOperation` manages the *concurrent* execution of one or more closures on the default global queue. This provides an object-oriented wrapper for apps that are already using an `OperationQueue` (discussed in the next chapter) and don't want to create a separate `DispatchQueue` as well.

Being an `Operation`, it can take advantage of **KVO** (Key-Value Observing) notifications, dependencies and everything else that an `Operation` provides.

What's not immediately apparent from the name of the class is that `BlockOperation` manages a **group** of closures. It acts similar to a dispatch group in that it marks itself as being finished when all of the closures have finished. The example above shows adding a single closure to the operation. You can, however, add multiple items, as you'll see in a moment.

> **Note**: Tasks in a `BlockOperation` run concurrently. If you need them to run serially, submit them to a private `DispatchQueue` or set up dependencies.

Multiple Block Operations

In the starter materials for this chapter, you'll find a playground named **BlockOperation.playground**. This playground provides a default `duration` function for timing your code, which you'll use in a moment.

When you want to add additional closures to the `BlockOperation`, you'll call the `addExecutionBlock` method and simply pass in a new closure. Use that method to print out a public service announcement, one word at a time. Paste the following code into your Playground:

```
let sentence = "Ray's courses are the best!"
let wordOperation = BlockOperation()

for word in sentence.split(separator: " ") {
  wordOperation.addExecutionBlock {
```

```
    print(word)
  }
}

wordOperation.start()
```

The above code splits the sentence apart on spaces, so you have an array of words. For each word, another closure is added to the operation. Thus, each word is printed as part of the `wordOperation`.

Display the console (Shift-Command-Y) and then run the playground. The sentence is printed to the console, one word per line, but the order is jumbled. Remember that a `BlockOperation` runs *concurrently*, not *serially*, and thus the order of execution is not deterministic.

Time to learn a little lesson in concurrency using the `duration` helper function I mentioned earlier.

Add a delay of two seconds right after the `print` call with the following line:

```
sleep(2)
```

Next, wrap the `start` call with the built-in `duration` function:

```
duration {
  wordOperation.start()
}
```

Take a look at the total time displayed on the line where you call `duration`.

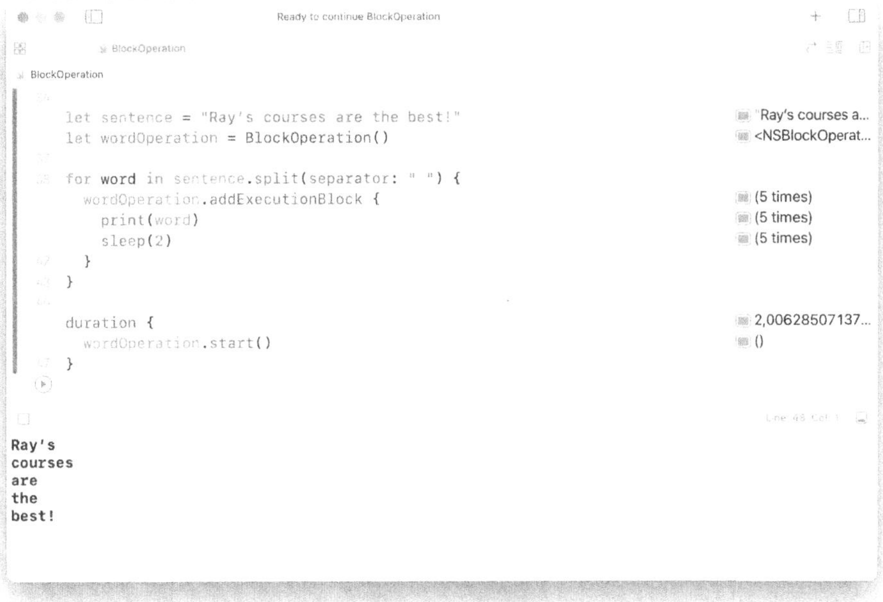

Even though each operation sleeps for two seconds, the total time of the operation itself is just over two seconds, not 10 seconds (five `prints` times two seconds each).

Remember that `BlockOperation` works similar to a `DispatchGroup` — that means it's gotta be easy to know when all the operations have completed, right?

If you provide a `completionBlock` closure, then it will be executed once all of the closures added to the block operation have finished. Add this code to your playground, before you call `duration`, and run it again to see the results:

```
wordOperation.completionBlock = {
  print("Thank you for your patronage!")
}
```

Subclassing Operation

`BlockOperation` is great for simple tasks but if performing more complex work, or for reusable components, you'll want to subclass `Operation` yourself.

Open up **Concurrency.xcodeproj** from the starter folder inside this chapter's download materials. Build and run the project and tap on the **Show Tilt Shift** button at the top of the screen.

You'll see an example of what you'll work with over the next few chapters. The image displayed at the top of the screen is the source image. After a few moments of processing, the **tilt shifted** image will appear below it.

Tilt shifting is a technique used on images to alter their depth of field. If you compare the two images, you'll see the the center of the bottom image is still in focus, but everything around it is blurred.

The example project provides a **TiltShiftFilter.swift** file, which is a subclass of `CIFilter`. Note that it works fine for educational purposes as the code is very clear and easy to follow, but it's far from optimal in terms of performance. If you need to use tilt shifting in a real application, there are far better solutions available.

If you jumped ahead and tapped on the **Show Table** button, you were probably pretty disappointed to just get an empty table view! Time to build that out.

Tilt Shift the Wrong Way

Since, according to Master Yoda, "The greatest teacher, failure is," you'll first implement the tilt shift the naive way most first-timers would attempt.

As mentioned earlier, you can see how the tilt shift is performed by taking a look at **TiltShiftFilter.swift**. If you're not familiar with Core Image, check out "Core Image Tutorial: Getting Started" (https://www.kodeco.com/30195423-core-image-tutorial-getting-started). While not specifically required to continue following along, this may be helpful to understand how filters work in the examples that follow.

The sample project provides ten images in its Asset Catalog for you to use. They're simply named **0** through **9** for ease of use. Open **ImageView.swift** in Xcode's editor window and add the following code to `tiltShiftImage`:

```
let name = "\(rowNumber).png"
let uiImage = UIImage(named: name)!
```

This will grab the image from the Asset Catalog. Next, add the following code to filter the image:

```
print("Tilt shifting image \(name)")

guard
  let filter = TiltShiftFilter(image: uiImage, radius: 3),
  let output = filter.outputImage
else {
  print("Failed to tilt shift \(name)")
  return
}
```

You'll try to filter the image using `TiltShiftFilter`, and if everything works out, you should get an output image. If something goes wrong, you'll print out an error message. The output image is of type `CIImage`. In order to display it, you need to convert it to `UIImage` and then to `Image`.

Add the following code:

```
print("Generating UIImage for \(name)")
let fromRect = CGRect(origin: .zero, size: uiImage.size)
guard let cgImage = CIContext().createCGImage(output, from:
fromRect) else {
  print("No image generated")
  return
}

let result = UIImage(cgImage: cgImage)
```

```
image = Image(uiImage: result)
print("Displaying \(name)")
```

You pass the output back through a `CIContext` to turn it back to a `CGImage`, then convert that to a `UIImage`.

> **Note**: Your phone will run Core Image operations an order of magnitude faster than an Intel-cpu Mac will. If you're running on the simulator, change the number of rows in the table view from 10 to two. I strongly suggest you test directly on your iOS device!

For the purposes of this demo, if using your Mac, those `print` statements are critical, so be sure that Xcode's console is showing (⇧ + ⌘ + Y) and then build and run the project.

Once the app starts up, tap on the **Show Table** button and watch the console window. Depending on the speed of your device or simulator, you'll see that the filtering takes a bit of time. If you scroll the table view, you'll observe stutters while the app tries to perform the tilt shift filter.

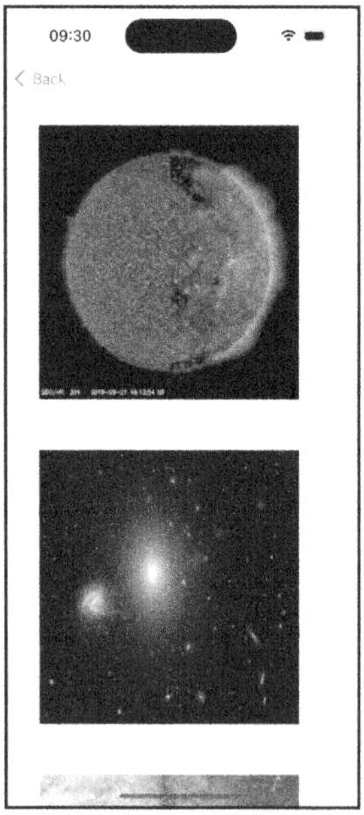

For a smoother experience, you'll have to move the tilt shifting off the main thread and perform it in the background, so let's do that.

Tilt Shift Almost Correctly

It should come as no surprise that the Core Image operations should be placed into an `Operation` subclass at this point. You're going to need both an input and an output image, so you'll create those two properties. The input image should never change so it makes sense to pass it to the initializer and make it private.

Create a new Swift file called **TiltShiftOperation.swift** and replace its content with the following:

```
import SwiftUI

final class TiltShiftOperation: Operation {
  var outputImage: UIImage?

  private let inputImage: UIImage

  init(image: UIImage) {
    inputImage = image
    super.init()
  }
}
```

In the **ImageView.swift** file, you created an instance of `CIContext` for every image, which is a bad thing to do. `CIContext` should be reused when possible, and Apple's documentation explicitly states that the `CIContext` is thread-safe, so you can make it `static`.

Add the `context` property to your class, right at the start of the class:

```
private static let context = CIContext()
```

All that's left to do now is override the `main` method, which is the method that will be invoked when your operation starts. Most of the code is similar to what you just wrote, with a few minor tweaks:

```
override func main() {
  guard
    let filter = TiltShiftFilter(image: inputImage, radius: 3),
    let output = filter.outputImage
  else {
    print("Failed to generate tilt shift image")
    return
  }

  let fromRect = CGRect(origin: .zero, size: inputImage.size)
  guard let cgImage = TiltShiftOperation.context.createCGImage(
```

```
      output, from: fromRect) else {
      print("No image generated")
      return
    }

    outputImage = UIImage(cgImage: cgImage)
  }
```

Notice that all print statements have been removed and the `context` references the `static` property, but other than that, things work the same way. If the filter is applied successfully, then the `outputImage` will be a non-`nil` value. If anything fails, it will stay `nil`.

All that's left to do now is to switch `ImageView` to utilize your new operation. If you want to manually run an operation, you can call its `start` method. Go back to **ImageView.swift** and replace `tiltShitImage` with this code:

```
private func tiltShiftImage() {
  print("Filtering")
  let op = TiltShiftOperation(image: UIImage(named: "\
(rowNumber).png")!)
  op.start()

  if let outputImage = op.outputImage {
    print("Updating image")
    image = Image(uiImage: outputImage)
  }

  print("Done")
}
```

Before you build and run the app again, take a moment to consider the changes you've made and their impact on the end user's experience. Build and run, now.

Did reality meet your expectations? Were you surprised there were no performance gains between this version of the app and the previous version? When you call the `start` method directly on an operation, you're performing a **synchronous** call on the **current thread** (i.e., the main thread). So while the code has been refactored into an `Operation` subclass, you're not yet taking advantage of the concurrency opportunities provided therein.

> **Note**: Besides the fact that calling `start` runs the operation on the current thread, it can also lead to an exception if the operation is not yet ready to be started. Generally, you shouldn't call `start` manually, unless you really know what you're doing!

In the next chapter, you'll begin to truly utilize the benefits of `Operation` and resolve that synchronous issue.

Chapter 7: Operation Queues

The real power of operations begins to appear when you let an `OperationQueue` handle your operations. Just like with GCD's `DispatchQueue`, `OperationQueue` is what you use to manage the scheduling of an `Operation` and the maximum number of operations that can run simultaneously.

`OperationQueue` allows you to add work in three separate ways:

- Pass an `Operation`.
- Pass a closure.
- Pass an array of `Operations`.

If you implemented the project from the previous chapter, you saw that an operation by itself is a synchronous task. While you could dispatch it asynchronously to a GCD queue to move it off the main thread, you'll want, instead, to add it to an `OperationQueue` to gain the full concurrency benefits of operations.

OperationQueue Management

The operation queue executes operations that are **ready**, according to quality of service values and any dependencies the operation has. Once you've added an `Operation` to the queue, it will run until it has completed or been canceled. You'll learn about dependencies and canceling operations in future chapters.

Once you've added an `Operation` to an `OperationQueue`, you can't add that same `Operation` to any other `OperationQueue`. `Operation` instances are **one and done** tasks, which is why you make them into subclasses so that you can execute them multiple times, if necessary.

Waiting for Completion

If you look under the hood of `OperationQueue`, you'll notice a method called `waitUntilAllOperationsAreFinished`. It does exactly what its name suggests: Whenever you find yourself wanting to call that method, in your head, replace the word **wait** with **block** in the method name. Calling it blocks the current thread, meaning that you must never call this method on the main UI thread.

If you find yourself needing this method, then you should set up a private serial `DispatchQueue` wherein you can safely call this blocking method. If you don't need to wait for all operations to complete, but just a set of operations, then you can, instead, use `addOperations(_:waitUntilFinished:)` on `OperationQueue`.

Quality of Service

An `OperationQueue` behaves like a `DispatchGroup` in that you can add operations with different quality of service values and they'll run according to the corresponding priority. If you need a refresher on the different quality of service levels, refer back to Chapter 3, "Queues & Threads."

The default quality of service level of an operation queue is `.background`. While you can set the `qualityOfService` property on the operation queue, keep in mind that it might be overridden by the quality of service that you've set on the individual operations managed by the queue.

Pausing the Queue

You can pause the dispatch queue by setting `isSuspended` to `true`. In-flight operations will continue to run but newly added operations will not be scheduled until you change `isSuspended` back to `false`.

Maximum Number of Operations

Sometimes you'll want to limit the number of operations which are running at a single time. By default, the dispatch queue will run as many jobs as your device is capable of handling at once. If you wish to limit that number, simply set the `maxConcurrentOperationCount` property on the dispatch queue. If you set the `maxConcurrentOperationCount` to `1`, then you've effectively created a serial queue.

Underlying DispatchQueue

Before you add any operations to an `OperationQueue`, you can specify an existing `DispatchQueue` as the `underlyingQueue`. If you do so, keep in mind that the quality of service of the dispatch queue will override any value you set for the operation queue's quality of service.

> **Note**: Do not specify the main queue as the underlying queue!

Fix the Previous Project

In the previous chapter, you set up an operation to handle the tilt shift, but it ran synchronously. Now that you're familiar with `OperationQueue`, you'll modify that project to work properly. You can either continue with your existing project or open up **TiltShift.xcodeproj** from this chapter's starter materials.

Updating the Table

Head over to **TableView.swift**. In order to add operations to a queue, you need to create one. Add the following property to the top of the class:

```
@State private var queue = OperationQueue()
```

Next, change the call to `ImageView` so that it takes the operation queue, and uses better parameter names:

```
ImageView(in: queue, for: rowNumber)
```

Now edit **ImageView.swift** to add a new property, as well as an initializer:

```
let queue: OperationQueue

init(in queue: OperationQueue, for rowNumber: Int) {
  self.rowNumber = rowNumber
  self.queue = queue
}
```

At this point you're ready to execute the tilt shift operation inside of the operation queue. Replace everything in `tiltShiftImage` after creating the operation with the following:

```
// 1
op.completionBlock = {
  // 2
  if let outputImage = op.outputImage {
    // 3
    DispatchQueue.main.async {
      print("Updating image")
      image = Image(uiImage: outputImage)
    }
  }
}

// 4
queue.addOperation(op)
```

Here's what's happening:

1. When the operation completes, the completion handler will be executed.
2. You determine whether an image was generated, as before.
3. The completion handler runs on a separate thread, so you need to dispatch back to the main queue before performing any UI updates.
4. Instead of calling `start`, you enqueue the operation so it runs when it can.

Now, the queue will be starting and completing it the operation for you. Additionally, the queue runs in the background by default, so you won't be blocking the main thread anymore.

When the operation completes, the `completionBlock` is called with no arguments, and it expects no return value. You'll immediately want to dispatch your code back to the main UI thread.

As soon as you add an operation to an operation queue, the job will be scheduled. Now there's no longer a reason to call `op.start()`.

Remember to update the `previews` to pass the proper parameters:

```
ImageView(in: OperationQueue(), for: Int.random(in: 0..<10))
```

Build and run the app and try scrolling the table again.

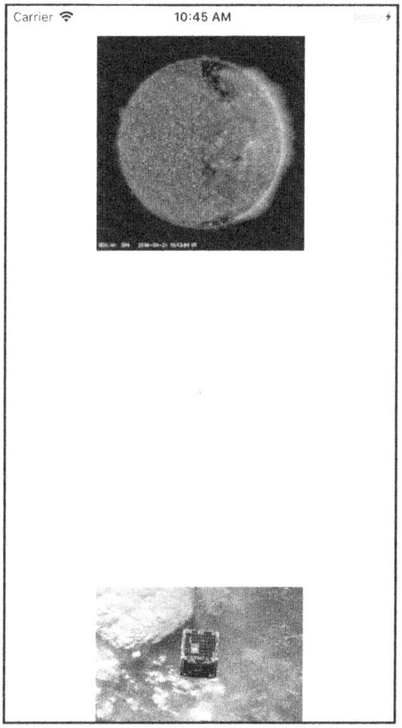

Now that your code is running in an asynchronous manner, the table scrolling is much smoother. While making such a change doesn't do anything to improve the performance of the code being run via the operation, it does ensure that the UI isn't locked up or choppy.

You may be thinking to yourself, "How is this any different than just doing it with GCD?" Right now, there really isn't a difference. But, in the next couple of chapters, you'll expand on the power of operations, and the reason for the changes will become clear.

Where to Go From Here?

The table currently loads and filters every image every time the cell is displayed. Think about how you might implement a caching solution so that the performance is even better.

The project is coming along nicely, but it is using static images, which usually won't be the case for production-worthy projects. In the next chapter, you'll take a look at network operations.

Chapter 8: Asynchronous Operations

Up to this point, your operations have been synchronous, which works very well with the `Operation` class' state machine. When the operation transitions to the `isReady` state, the system knows that it can start searching for an available thread.

Once the scheduler has found a thread on which to run the operation, the operation will transition to the `isExecuting` state. At that point, your code executes and completes, and the state then becomes `isFinished`.

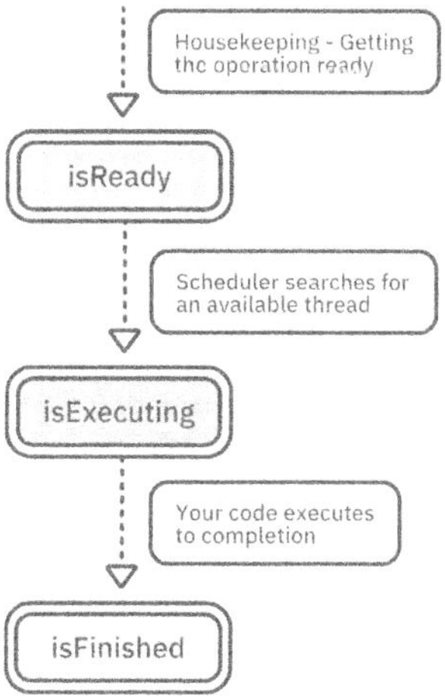

How would that work with an *asynchronous* operation, though? When the `main` method of the operation executes, it will kick off your asynchronous task, and then `main` exits. The state of the operation can't switch to `isFinished` at that point because the asynchronous method likely has yet to complete.

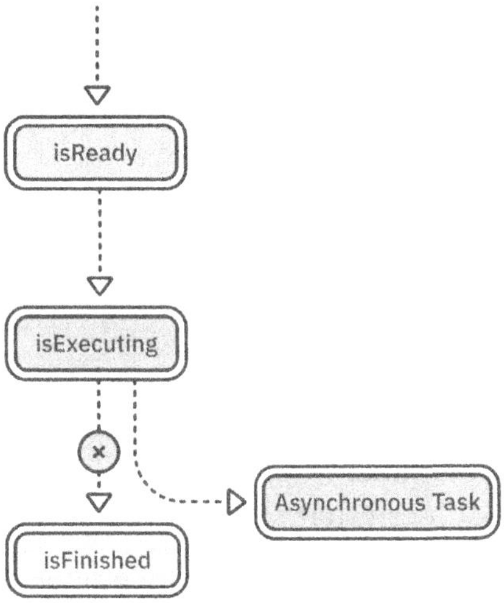

Asynchronous Operations

It's possible to wrap an asynchronous method into an operation, but it takes a bit more work on your part. You'll need to manage the state changes manually as the operation can't determine automatically when the task has finished executing. To make matters worse, the state properties are all read-only!

If you're ready to throw in the towel, don't worry. Managing the states is actually quite simple to accomplish. In fact, you will now create a base class that all asynchronous operations you use will inherit from so you never have to do it again. No, we don't know why this class isn't part of the framework.

AsyncOperation

In the download materials for this chapter, open **AsyncAddOperation.playground** in the **starter** folder. You can ignore the compilation error as you'll resolve it in a moment when you add some code.

State Tracking

Since the state of an operation is read-only, you'll first want to give yourself a way to track changes in a read-write manner, so create a `State` enumeration at the top of the file:

```
extension AsyncOperation {
  enum State: String {
    case ready, executing, finished

    fileprivate var keyPath: String {
      return "is\(rawValue.capitalized)"
    }
  }
}
```

Back in Chapter 6, "Operations," I mentioned that the `Operation` class uses **KVO notifications**. When the `isExecuting` state changes, for example, a KVO notification will be sent. The states you set yourself don't start with the '**is**' prefix though, and, per the Swift style guide, `enum` entries should be lowercased.

The `keyPath` computed property you wrote is what helps support the aforementioned KVO notifications. When you ask for the `keyPath` of your current `State`, it will capitalize the first letter of the state's value and prefix with the text **is**. Thus, when your state is set to `executing`, the `keyPath` will return `isExecuting`, which matches the property on the `Operation` base class.

Notice the `fileprivate` modifier. You thought the need to ever use that monstrosity went away with the fixes in Swift 4, didn't you? This is a case in which it's still helpful. The `keyPath` needs to be available to this entire file but not externally. If you just made it `private`, then it wouldn't be visible outside of the `enum` itself.

Be aware that the scoping is now the entire *file*, so you'll want to make sure the class lives in a file of its own for production code.

Now that you have the type of your state created, you'll need a variable to hold the state. Because you need to send the appropriate KVO notifications when you change the value, you'll attach property observers to the property. Add the following code to `AsyncOperation`:

```
var state = State.ready {
  willSet {
    willChangeValue(forKey: newValue.keyPath)
    willChangeValue(forKey: state.keyPath)
  }
  didSet {
```

```
    didChangeValue(forKey: oldValue.keyPath)
    didChangeValue(forKey: state.keyPath)
  }
}
```

By default, your `state` is `ready`. When you change the value of `state`, you'll actually end up sending four KVO notifications! Take a minute to see if you can understand what is happening and why there are four entries there instead of just two.

Consider the case in which the state is currently `ready` and you are updating to `executing`. `isReady` will become `false`, while `isExecuting` will become `true`. These four KVO notifications will be sent:

1. Will change for `isReady`.
2. Will change for `isExecuting`.
3. Did change for `isReady`.
4. Did change for `isExecuting`.

The `Operation` base class needs to know that both the `isExecuting` and `isReady` properties are changing.

Base Properties

Now that you have a way to track state changes and signal that a change was in fact performed, you'll need to override the base class' instances of those methods to use your state instead. Add these three overrides to the class:

```
override var isReady: Bool {
  super.isReady && state == .ready
}
override var isExecuting: Bool { state == .executing }
override var isFinished: Bool { state == .finished }
```

> **Note**: It's critical that you include a check to the base class' `isReady` as your code isn't aware of everything that goes on while the scheduler determines whether or not it is ready to find your operation a thread to use.

The final property to override is simply to specify that you are in fact using an asynchronous operation. Add the following piece of code:

```
override var isAsynchronous: Bool { true }
```

Starting the Operation

All that's left to do is implement the `start` method. Whether you manually execute an operation or let the operation queue do it for you, the `start` method is what gets called first, and then it is responsible for calling `main`.

Add the following code to the end of the class:

```
override func start() {
  main()
  state = .executing
}
```

> **Note**: Notice this code doesn't invoke `super.start()`. The official documentation (https://apple.co/2YcJvEh) clearly mentions that you **must not** call super at any time when overriding `start`.

Those two lines probably look backwards to you. They're really not. Because you're performing an asynchronous task, the `main` method is going to almost immediately return, thus you have to manually put the state back to `.executing` so the operation knows it is still in progress.

> **Note**: There's a piece missing from the above code. Chapter 10, "Canceling Operations," will talk about cancelable operations, and that code needs to be in any `start` method. It's left out here to avoid confusion.

If Swift had a concept of an abstract class, which couldn't be directly instantiated, you would mark this class as abstract. In other words, never directly use this class. You should always subclass `AsyncOperation`!

Math Is Fun!

Take a look at the rest of the code that was provided for you in the playground. Nothing should be new to you, as long as you already worked through the chapters on GCD in this book. If you run the playground with the console displayed (Shift-Command-Y), you'll see the numbers have been added together properly.

The key detail in the `AsyncSumOperation` to pay attention to is that you must manually set the `state` of the operation to `.finished` when the asynchronous task completes. If you forget to change the state then the operation will never be marked as complete, and you'll have what is known as an infinite loop.

> **Note**: Be sure to always set the `state` to `.finished` when your asynchronous method completes.

Networked TiltShift

Time to get back to your image filtering. So far, you've used a hardcoded list of images. Wouldn't it be great if the images came from the network instead? Performing a network operation is simply an asynchronous task! Now that you have a way to turn an asynchronous task into an operation, let's get to it!

The starter project for this chapter, located in the **starter/TiltShift** folder, continues the project you've been building but includes two new files, as well as a couple other small changes.

NetworkImageOperation

Create a new Swift file named **NetworkImageOperation**. You're going to make this do more than specifically needed for the project but this way you'll have a reusable component for any other project you work on.

The general requirements for the operation are as follows:

1. Should take either a `String` representing a URL or an actual `URL`.
2. Should download the data at the specified URL.
3. If a `URLSession`-type completion handler is provided, use that instead of decoding.
4. If successful, there's no completion handler and it's an image; should set an optional `UIImage` value.

The first two requirements should be pretty obvious. The third and fourth are to give maximum flexibility to the caller. In some cases, as with this project, you just want to grab the decoded `UIImage` and be done. Other projects though may require custom processing. For example, you may care about what the specific error is, whether the HTTP header has a valid `Content-Type` header, etc.

Begin by subclassing `AsyncOperation` and declaring the variables that the class will need. Create a new Swift file called **NetworkImageOperation.swift** and add the following code:

```
import UIKit

typealias ImageOperationCompletion = ((Data?, URLResponse?,
Error?) -> Void)?

final class NetworkImageOperation: AsyncOperation {
  var image: UIImage?

  private let url: URL
  private let completion: ImageOperationCompletion

}
```

The `completion` signature is the same signature used by `URLSession` methods, just turned into an optional. To meet requirements 1 and 2, you'll need to define appropriate initializers. Add the following code inside your new class:

```
init(url: URL, completion: ImageOperationCompletion = nil) {
  self.url = url
  self.completion = completion

  super.init()
}

convenience init?(string: String, completion:
ImageOperationCompletion = nil) {
  guard let url = URL(string: string) else { return nil }
  self.init(url: url, completion: completion)
}
```

It's probably not the normal case that someone will want to explicitly handle the HTTP return data themselves, so it makes sense to default the completion handler to `nil`. Passing an actual `URL` is the "designated initializer" and, thus, you're declaring a convenience initializer that takes a string instead. Note how that constructor is itself an optional. If you pass a string that isn't able to be converted to a URL, then the constructor will return `nil`.

Housekeeping, check! Now for the actual work of the operation. Override `main` and start a new `URLSession` task, as you would usually use `URLSession`. Add below your initializers:

```
override func main() {
  URLSession.shared.dataTask(with: url) {
    [weak self] data, response, error in

  }.resume()
}
```

Since this is an asynchronous operation, it's always possible that the object will be removed before the data download happens, so you need to be sure you can retain `self`, thus using `weak` capture group.

Now, it's time to handle the completed task. Add the following code inside the completion closure:

```
guard let self else { return }

defer { self.state = .finished }

if let completion = self.completion {
  completion(data, response, error)
  return
}

guard error == nil, let data = data else { return }

self.image = UIImage(data: data)
```

Using `defer` ensures that the operation is eventually marked as complete. There are already three possible exit paths in the current method, plus you never know what changes you might make in the future. Putting the `defer` statement right up front makes it bullet proof.

Meeting requirements 3 and 4 is as simple as checking for whether or not the caller has provided a completion handler. If they have provided a completion handler, you just pass the processing responsibility to it and exit. If not, then you can decode the image.

Note that there's no need to throw exceptions or return any type of error condition. If anything fails, then the `image` property will be `nil`, and the caller will know something went wrong.

Using NetworkImageOperation

Head back over to **TableView.swift**. In order to get the list of URLs that you'll be able to display, the starter project included a `loadPhotoUrls` method for you.

That's the standard Swift mechanism for reading the contents of a .plist file and converting the strings to actual `URL` objects. You might not have seen `compactMap` before. It works just like `map` does, just for an array of Optional values. It excludes any `nil` items and returns only unwrapped, non-optional values. In this case, that means the `urls` array will just contain valid `URL` objects.

Notice that the `body` now calls `ImageView` by passing in a URL instead of a row number.

Edit **ImageView.swift** and replace the `TiltShiftOperation` call with `NetworkImageOperation`:

```
let op = NetworkImageOperation(url: url)
```

The `TiltShiftOperation` class used `outputImage` as the result variable, whereas `NetworkImageOperation` uses just `image`, so replace the following line:

```
if let outputImage = op.outputImage {
```

With:

```
if let outputImage = op.image {
```

At this point, you can build and run the app and scroll through a large list of interesting images.

The scrolling will be nice and smooth as the UI isn't hung at any point during the network operation.

Where to Go From Here?

You've now got reusable components for both network image downloads as well as tilt shift filtering. Wouldn't it be nice to be able to use both at once? The next chapter will show you how to link those two together and finally provide the "*aha*" moment as to why you're using operations instead of sticking with Grand Central Dispatch.

Chapter 9: Operation Dependencies

In this chapter, you're going to learn about **dependencies** between operations. Making one operation dependent on another provides two specific benefits for the interactions between operations:

1. Ensures that the dependent operation does not begin before the prerequisite operation has completed.
2. Provides a clean way to pass data from the first operation to the second operation automatically.

Enabling dependencies between operations is one of the primary reasons you'll find yourself choosing to use an `Operation` over GCD.

Modular Design

Consider the tilt shift project you've been creating. You now have an operation that will download from the network, as well as an operation that will perform the tilt shift. You could instead create a single operation that performs both tasks, but that's not a good architectural design.

Classes should ideally perform a single task, enabling reuse within and across projects. If you had built the networking code into the tilt shift operation directly, then it wouldn't be usable for an already-bundled image. While you could add many initialization parameters specifying whether or not the image would be provided or downloaded from the network, that bloats the class. Not only does it increase the long-term maintenance of the class — imagine switching from URLSession to Alamofire — it also increases the number of test cases which have to be designed.

Specifying Dependencies

Adding or removing a dependency requires just a single method call on the **dependent** operation. Consider a fictitious example in which you'd download an image, decrypt it and then run the resultant image through a tilt shift:

```
let networkOp = NetworkImageOperation()
let decryptOp = DecryptOperation()
let tiltShiftOp = TiltShiftOperation()

decryptOp.addDependency(op: networkOp)
tiltShiftOp.addDependency(op: decryptOp)
```

If you needed to remove a dependency for some reason, you'd simply call the obviously named method, removeDependency(op:):

```
tiltShiftOp.removeDependency(op: decryptOp)
```

The Operation class also provides a read-only property, dependencies, which will return an array of Operations, which are marked as dependencies for the given operation.

Avoiding the Pyramid of Doom

Dependencies have the added side effect of making the code much simpler to read. If you tried to write three chained operations together using GCD, you'd end up with a pyramid of doom. Consider the following **pseudo-code** for how you might have to represent the previous example with GCD:

```
let network = NetworkClass()
network.onDownloaded { raw in
  guard let raw else { return }

  let decrypt = DecryptClass(raw)
  decrypt.onDecrypted { decrypted in
    guard let decrypted else { return }

    let tilt = TiltShiftClass(decrypted)
    tilt.onTiltShifted { tilted in
      guard let tilted else { return }
    }
  }
}
```

Which one is going to be easier to understand and maintain for the junior developer who takes over your project once you move on to bigger and better things? Consider also that the example provided doesn't take into account the retain cycles or error checking that real code would have to handle properly.

Watch Out for Deadlock

In Chapter 5, "Concurrency Problems," you learned about deadlock. Any time a task is dependent on another, you introduce the possibility of deadlock, if you aren't careful. Picture in your mind — better yet graph out — the dependency chain. If the graph draws a straight line, then there's no possibility of deadlock.

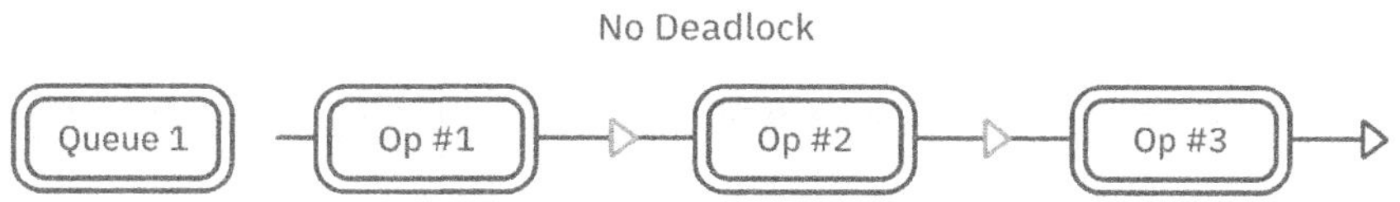

It's completely valid to have the operations from one operation queue depend on an operation from another operation queue. Even when you do that, as long as there are no loops, you're still safe from deadlock.

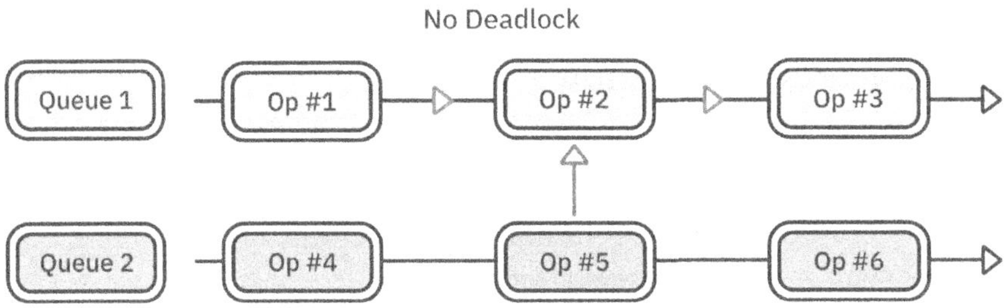

If, however, you start seeing loops, you've almost certainly run into a deadlock situation.

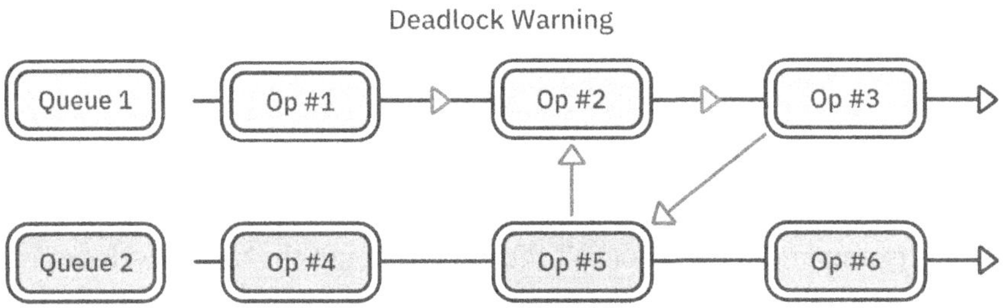

In the previous image, you can see where the problem lies:

- Operation 2 can't start until operation 5 is done.
- Operation 5 can't start until operation 3 is done.
- Operation 3 can't start until operation 2 is done.

If you start and end with the same operation number in a cycle, you've hit deadlock. None of the operations will ever be executed. There's no silver-bullet solution to resolve a deadlock situation, and they can be hard to find if you don't map out your dependencies. If you run into such a situation, you have no choice but to re-architect the solution you've designed.

Passing Data Between Operations

Now that you've got a way to safely make one operation depend on another, there has to be a way to pass data between them. Enter the power of protocols. The `NetworkImageOperation` has an output property called `image`. What about the case, though, in which the property is called something else?

Part of the benefit to operations is the encapsulation and reusability they provide. You can't expect every person who writes an operation to call the output property `image`. Internally, to the class, there might have been a good reason to call it `foodImage`, for example.

Using Protocols

Here's what you're really saying: "When this operation finishes, if everything went well, I will provide you with an image of type `Image`."

As usual, open **TiltShift.xcodeproj** in the starter project folder that comes with this chapter's download materials and then create a new Swift file called **ImageDataProvider.swift**.

Add the following code to the file:

```
import UIKit

protocol ImageDataProvider {
  var image: UIImage? { get }
}
```

Any operation that has an output of a `UIImage` should implement that protocol. In this case, the property names match one-to-one, which makes life easier. Think about your `TiltShiftOperation`, though. Following `CIFilter` naming conventions you called that one `outputImage`. Both classes should conform to the `ImageDataProvider`.

Adding Extensions

Open up **NetworkImageOperation.swift** and add this code to the very bottom of the file:

```
extension NetworkImageOperation: ImageDataProvider {}
```

Since the class already contains the property exactly as defined by the protocol, there's nothing else you need to do. While you could have simply added `ImageDataProvider` to the class definition, the Swift Style Guide recommends the `extension` approach instead.

For `TiltShiftOperation`, there's a tiny bit more work to do. While you already have an output image, the name of the property isn't `image` as defined by the protocol.

Add the following code at the end of **TiltShiftOperation.swift**:

```
extension TiltShiftOperation: ImageDataProvider {
  var image: UIImage? { outputImage }
}
```

Remember that an extension can be placed anywhere, in any file. Since you created both operations, it makes sense of course to place the extension right alongside the class. You might be using a third-party framework, however, wherein you can't edit the source. If the operation it provides gives you an image, you can add the extension to it yourself in a file within your project, like **ThirdPartyOperation+Extension.swift**.

Searching for the Protocol

The `TiltShiftOperation` needs a `UIImage` as its input. Instead of just requiring the `inputImage` property be set, it can now check whether any of its dependencies provides a `UIImage` as output.

In **TiltShiftOperation.swift**, change the type of `inputImage` from `UIImage` to `UIImage?`.

Next, in `main()`, change the first `guard` statement to this:

```
let dependencyImage = dependencies
  .compactMap { ($0 as? ImageDataProvider)?.image }
  .first

guard
  let inputImage = inputImage ?? dependencyImage,
```

```
    let filter = TiltShiftFilter(image: inputImage, radius: 3),
    let output = filter.outputImage
  else {
    return
  }
```

In the above code, you try to unwrap either the input image directly provided to the operation or the dependency chain for something that will provide us an image, making sure it gave a non-`nil` image.

If neither of those worked, simply return without performing any work.

There's one last piece to making this all work. Because you now check the dependency chain for an image, there has to be a way to initialize a `TiltShiftOperation` without providing an input image. The simplest way to handle no input is by making the current constructor default the input image to `nil`.

Adjust your initializer to look as follows:

```
init(image: UIImage? = nil) {
  inputImage = image
  super.init()
}
```

Updating the ImageView

Head back over to **ImageView.swift** and see if you can update it to download the image, tilt shift it, and then assign it to the display.

For this to work, you'll need to add the download operation as a dependency of the tilt shift operation. In other words, the tilt shift *depends* on the download operation to get the image.

Replace the line in `tiltShiftImage` where you set and declare op with the following code:

```
let downloadOp = NetworkImageOperation(url: url)
let op = TiltShiftOperation()
op.addDependency(downloadOp)
```

Instead of having a single operation, you now have two operations and a dependency between them.

Finally, just before adding the operation to the queue, add the downloadOp:

```
queue.addOperation(downloadOp)
```

Even though you said that the tilt shift depends on the download, you still need to add both operations to the queue. The queue will keep track of dependencies and only start the tilt shift operation once the download is complete.

Build and run the app. You should see a list of tilt shifted images!

Custom Completion Handler

The code as currently written is using the default completionBlock provided by the Operation class. You're having to do a little extra work there to grab the image and dispatch back to the main queue. In a case like this, you may want to consider adding a custom completion block.

Back in **TiltShiftOperation.swift**, add a new optional class-level property at the top of the class to store a custom completion handler:

```
/// Callback which will be run *on the main thread*
/// when the operation completes.
var onImageProcessed: ((UIImage?) -> Void)?
```

Then, at the very end of the `main()` method, after assigning the `outputImage`, call that completion handler *on the main thread*:

```
if let onImageProcessed {
  DispatchQueue.main.async { [weak self] in
    guard let self else { return }
    onImageProcessed(outputImage)
  }
}
```

If you add that extra bit of code then back in **ImageView.swift**, in `tiltShiftImage`, you can replace the entire completion block code with this:

```
op.onImageProcessed = { uiImage in
  if let uiImage {
    image = Image(uiImage: uiImage)
  }
}
```

While there's no functional or performance difference from those changes, it does make working with your operation a bit nicer for the caller. You've removed confusion over any possible retain cycle and ensured that they're properly working on the main UI thread automatically.

It's very important that you **document** the fact that your completion handler is being run on the main UI thread instead of the operation queue's provided thread.

The end user needs to know you're switching threads on them so they don't do something that could impact the application.

Notice how there are three `/` characters in the comment shown. If you use that syntax, then Xcode will display that comment as the summary of the property in the Quick Help Inspector. Xcode supports limited styling as well, which means that the text *on the main thread* will actually be italicized in the help display.

Where to Go From Here?

Throughout this chapter, you've learned how to tie the start of one operation to the completion of another. Consider where, in your existing apps, you could implement operations and operation dependencies to better modularize your app and remove the Pyramid of Doom indentation that you've likely implemented.

Chapter 10: Canceling Operations

With an operation, you have the capability of canceling a running operation *as long as it's written properly*. This is very useful for long operations that can become irrelevant over time. For instance, the user might leave the screen or scroll away from a cell in a table view. There's no sense in continuing to load data or make complex calculations if the user isn't going to see the result.

The Magic of Cancel

Once you schedule an operation into an operation queue, you no longer have any control over it. The queue will schedule and manage the operation from then on. The one and only change you can make, once it's been added to the queue, is to call the `cancel` method of `Operation`.

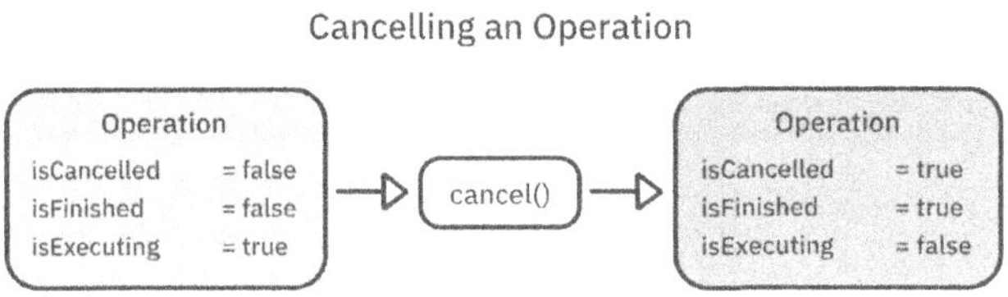

There's nothing magical about how canceling an operation works. If you send a request to an operation to stop running, then the `isCancelled` computed property will return `true`. Nothing else happens automatically! At first, it may seem strange that iOS doesn't stop the operation automatically, but it's really not.

What does *canceling* an operation mean to the OS?

- Should the operation simply throw an exception?
- Is there cleanup that needs to take place?
- Can a running network call be canceled?
- Is there a message to send server-side to let something else know the task stopped?
- If the operation stops, will data be corrupted?

With just the small list of issues presented in the bullets above, you can see why setting a flag identifying that cancellation has been *requested* is all that's possible automatically.

The default `start` implementation of `Operation` will first check to see whether the `isCancelled` flag is `true`, and exit immediately if it is.

Cancel and cancelAllOperations

The interface to cancel an operation is quite simple. If you just want to cancel a specific `Operation`, then you can call the `cancel` method. If, on the other hand, you wish to cancel all operations that are in an operation queue, then you should call the `cancelAllOperations` method defined on `OperationQueue`.

Updating AsyncOperation

In this chapter, you'll update the app you've been working on so that an image's operations are canceled when the user scrolls away from that image.

In Chapter 8, "Asynchronous Operations," you built the `AsyncOperation` base class. If you recall, there was a note with that code warning you that the provided implementation wasn't entirely complete. It's time to fix that!

The `start` method provided was written like so:

```
override func start() {
  main()
  state = .executing
}
```

If you're going to allow your operation to be cancelable — which you should always do unless you have a *very* good reason not to — then you need to check the `isCancelled` variable at appropriate locations. Open up the starter project from this chapter's download materials and edit **AsyncOperation.swift** to update `start`:

```
override func start() {
  if isCancelled {
    state = .finished
    return
  }

  main()
  state = .executing
}
```

After the above changes, it's now possible for your operation to be canceled before it's started.

Canceling a Running Operation

To support the cancellation of a running operation, you'll need to sprinkle checks for `isCancelled` throughout the operation's code. Obviously, more complex operations are going to be able to check in more places than something simple like your `NetworkImageOperation`.

Open up **NetworkImageOperation.swift** and in `main`, add a new `guard` statement right after the `defer`:

```
guard !self.isCancelled else { return }
```

For the network download, there's really no other location that you'd need to make the check. In fact, it's questionable whether or not you'd really want to make the check at all.

You've already spent the time to download the image from the network. Is it better to cancel and return no image, or let the image get created? There's no right or wrong answer. It's simply an architectural decision that you'll have to make based on the requirements of the project.

Next, add a way to cancel the network request while it's in progress. First, add a new property to the class:

```
private var task: URLSessionDataTask?
```

This will hold the network task while it's being run. Next, in `main`, assign the output of the `dataTask` call to `task`:

```
task = URLSession.shared.dataTask(with: url) {
```

Next, remove the call to `resume` at the end of that block. Instead, you're going to call `resume` on the `task` by adding the following at the end of `main`:

```
task?.resume()
```

Finally, you need to override `cancel` to make sure the task is canceled. Add the following method to the class:

```
override func cancel() {
  super.cancel()
  task?.cancel()
}
```

Now, the downloading can be canceled at any time.

It's time to allow canceling in **TiltShiftOperation.swift**. You'll probably want to place two checks in the `main` method. Just before setting the `fromRect` variable, make the first check:

```
guard !isCancelled else { return }
```

Once you've applied the tilt shift and grabbed the output image, that's a good point to stop before you then create the `CGImage`.

Next, just before setting `outputImage`, add the same check again.

```
guard !isCancelled else { return }
```

You've got a `CGImage` at this point but there's no value in converting it to a `UIImage` if a cancellation was requested. Some would argue for a third check, right after creating the `outputImage`, but that leads to the same question posed during the network operation: You've already done all the work, do you really want to stop now?

Now that you have a way to cancel the operation, it's time to hook this up to `ImageView` so that the operations are canceled when the user scrolls away.

Open up **ImageView.swift** and add the following property to the class:

```
@State private var operations: [Operation] = []
```

This is an array that will hold the operations for this specific image (both the downloading and tilt shifting). You need to store the operations because canceling is a method on the actual operation, so you need a way to grab it to cancel it.

In `tiltShiftImage`, just before adding the operations to the queue, store them:

```
operations = [downloadOp, tiltShiftOp]
```

Then, at the end of `body`, cancel the operations when the view disappears:

```
.onDisappear {
  operations.forEach { $0.cancel() }
}
```

Build and run the app.

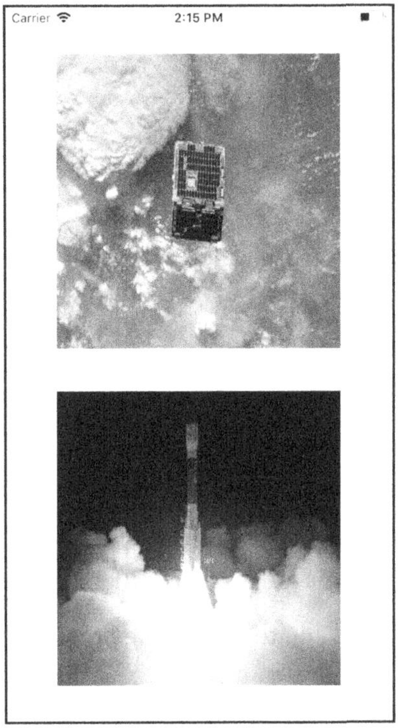

You probably won't notice a big difference, but now when you quickly scroll through the table view the app won't load and filter an image for each cell that quickly went past the screen. The downloads for the ones that went offscreen are canceled, saving the user's network traffic and battery life and making your app run faster.

Where to Go From Here?

Having to cancel an operation doesn't necessarily mean something negative happened. At times you cancel an operation because it's simply no longer necessary.

Section IV: Real-Life Concurrency

To wrap up this book, this section will be dedicated to showing you how you can use the knowledge you've accumulated throughout this book for real-life purposes.

In this section, you'll take a deeper dive into a common case where concurrency plays a huge role — Core Data — as well as learn about Apple's Thread Sanitizer, a great tool to debug and resolve concurrency issues and confusions.

Chapter 11: Core Data

Many of the iOS apps you'll develop are likely to use Core Data for data storage. While mixing concurrency and Core Data is no longer complicated in modern versions of iOS, there are still a couple of key concepts that you'll want to be aware of. Just like most of UIKit, Core Data is not thread safe.

> **Note**: This chapter assumes that you already know how to perform basic Core Data concepts such as searching, creating entities, etc... Please check out our book, Core Data by Tutorials (https://www.kodeco.com/books/core-data-by-tutorials) if you are new to Core Data.

NSManagedObjectContext Is Not Thread Safe

The `NSManagedObjectContext`, which gets created as part of an `NSPersistentContainer` from your `AppDelegate`, is tied to the main thread. As you've learned throughout the rest of this book, this means you can only use that context on the main UI thread. However, if you do so, you're going to negatively impact your user's experience.

There are two methods available on the `NSManagedObjectContext` class to help with concurrency:

- `perform(_:)`
- `performAndWait(_:)`

What both methods do is ensure that whatever action you pass to the closure is executed on the same queue that created the context. Notice how it's not "on the main thread." You might create your own context on another queue. These methods thus ensure that you are always executing against the proper thread and don't crash at runtime.

The only difference between the two is that the first is an asynchronous method, whereas the second is synchronous. It should be abnormal for you to perform Core Data tasks without utilizing either of these methods. Even though you might know you're on the proper thread already, you might refactor your code in the future and forget to wrap the Core Data calls at that point in time. Save yourself the headache and use them right from the start!

Importing Data

When your app starts, one of the first goals it frequently has is to contact the server and download any new data. Once the network operation completes, an expensive compare and import cycle will have to take place. However, you don't need to create an entire `Operation` for this common task. Core Data's `NSPersistentContainer` provides `performBackgroundTask(_:)` which will help you out:

```
PersistenceController.shared.container.performBackgroundTask
{ context in
  for json in jsonDataFromServer {
    let obj = MyEntity(context: context)
```

```
    obj.populate(from: json)
  }

  do {
    try context.save()
  } catch {
    fatalError("Failed to save context")
  }
}
```

Notice how the closure argument is an `NSManagedObjectContext`. Core Data will generate a new context on a private queue for you to work with so that you don't have to worry about any concurrency issues. Be sure not to use any other context in the closure or you'll run into tough to debug runtime issues.

If you've worked with Core Data and concurrency in the past, you'll see that `performBackgroundTask` is a convenience method for this previously required song and dance:

```
let childContext =
NSManagedObjectContext(concurrencyType: .privateQueueConcurrency
Type)
childContext.parent = persistentContainer.viewContext

childContext.perform {
  ...
}
```

No lying, now: How many times have you written the preceding code and forgotten to set the `parent` context properly?

Using NSAsynchronousFetchRequest

When you use a `FetchRequest` to query Core Data, the operation is synchronous. If you're just grabbing a single object, that's perfectly acceptable. When you're performing a time-consuming query, such as retrieving data to populate a `List`, then you'll prefer to perform the query asynchronously. Using `NSAsynchronousFetchRequest` is the obvious solution.

Construct the fetch request as you normally would but then pass that fetch request as the first parameter to the constructor of `NSAsynchronousFetchRequest`. The second parameter is a closure to be executed when the fetch completes. The closure takes a single argument of type `NSAsynchronousFetchResult`.

> **Note**: An asynchronous fetch request must be run in a private background queue.

Running your asynchronous fetch request in a private background queue is easily accomplished via the `newBackgroundContext` method of your persistent container, like so:

```
let ageKeyPath = #keyPath(Person.age)

let fetchRequest = Person.fetchRequest()
fetchRequest.predicate = NSPredicate(format: "%K > 13",
ageKeyPath)

let asyncFetch = NSAsynchronousFetchRequest(fetchRequest:
fetchRequest) {
  result in

  guard let people = result.finalResult else {
    return
  }

  DispatchQueue.main.async {
    self.people = people
  }
}

do {
  let backgroundContext =
PersistenceController.shared.container.newBackgroundContext()
  try backgroundContext.execute(asyncFetch)
} catch let error {
  // handle the error
}
```

Sharing an NSManagedObject

You can't share an `NSManagedObject` — or a subclass — between threads. Sure, you *can*, and more often than not it will *seem* to work, but your app is going to break, so don't do it!

That doesn't mean you can't effectively use Core Data if your app is written to fully utilize multiple threads. If two separate threads both need access to the same object, you must pass the `NSManagedObjectId` instead of the actual `NSManagedObject`. You can get the `NSManagedObjectId` via the `objectID` property. A common situation wherein you'd need to use the same entity across multiple threads is when you post a notification after creating or updating the entity.

It's incredibly easy to get the entity you want based on an ID:

```
let objectId = someEntity.objectID

DispatchQueue.main.async { [weak self] in
  guard let self else { return }

  let myEntity = self.managedObjectContext.object(with:
objectId)
  self.address = myEntity.address
}
```

Using ConcurrencyDebug

To help protect yourself from sharing an `NSManagedObject` across threads, you can enable a runtime debug flag by editing the project' scheme and passing a runtime argument.

Add `-com.apple.CoreData.ConcurrencyDebug 1` to your app's scheme to catch calling Core Data methods on the wrong thread in the debugger. While adding the debugging flag provides an extra level of safety, it also comes at a large performance cost. You'll find that leaving the flag enabled is usually a bad idea as it makes your app look less performant, which is the opposite of what you're trying to do! However, you should periodically perform your full suite of tests with the flag enabled to catch any mistakes.

In this chapter project's download materials, open the **Concurrency.xcodeproj** project. In **ContentView.swift** you'll see there are two aptly named methods defined, both match the callback signature for an `NSNotification`:

- `doItTheRightWay(note:)`
- `doItTheWrongWay(note:)`

The project is currently set to pass the actual `NSManagedObject` to the notification, which, of course, you just learned is really bad! Build and run the app. You can tap on the **Generate** button a bunch of times, and you'll likely be told how many Core Data entities were generated.

What's going on here, though? I just told you the app is written incorrectly, yet everything works just fine! Edit the scheme of your app now and put a checkmark next to the concurrency debug argument so that it' enabled and then run the app again.

> **Note**: The current version of Xcode broke the `ConcurrencyDebug` flag, and it no longer catches the issue. If you repeatedly press the Generate button, you'll eventually get a crash, or see the **This would crash** message.

This time the progress bar will run to completion as normal but, instead of getting a text message telling you how many entities were created, you'll notice that you crashed in Xcode. Using the extra debugging provided by the runtime argument caused Xcode to notice that you crossed threads with an `NSManagedObject` and so it aborted with an **EXC_BAD_INSTRUCTION** exception. Running in debug mode catches your bad memory usage.

Head back to `MainViewController` and change this line at the top of the class:

```
private let passActualObject = true
```

To this:

```
private let passActualObject = false
```

Rebuild and rerun your app. This time you won't crash. You'll see the difference between the two methods is that the `doItTheRightWay(note:)` method is looking up the entity properly based on the `objectID` and not taking an actual object.

Hopefully this small example shows you how important it is to run with the extra debugging enabled long before you ship your app to production. Just because the app normally works doesn't mean that it always will if you cross thread boundaries. On a real device, performing normal daily tasks, you'll eventually hit memory corruption if you try to share an `NSManagedObject` across threads.

Where to Go From Here?

Hopefully, the preceding few pages have shown you that it's pretty easy to work with Core Data in a thread safe way. If you previously shied away from this great framework because it was hard to use concurrently, now is the time to take another look!

If you'd like to know more about the intricacies of Core Data, please check out our book, Core Data by Tutorials (https://www.kodeco.com/books/core-data-by-tutorials).

Chapter 12: Thread Sanitizer

By the time you reach this chapter, you should be a whiz at concurrent programming.

However, just because your app *seems* to run correctly doesn't mean you took care of various concurrency and threading related edge cases. In this chapter you'll learn how to utilize Xcode's built-in **Thread Sanitizer** to discover races and before you deploy to the App Store.

Why the Sanitizer?

As discussed in Chapter 5, "Concurrency Problems," you know how important it is to keep all accesses to a variable on the same thread to avoid data races. Depending on how your app is structured, or the architecture of a third-party library that you're using, it can be hard to tell if you're crossing a thread boundary.

The Thread Sanitizer, commonly referred to as TSan, is a tool Apple provides as part of the LLVM compiler. TSan allows you to identify when multiple threads attempt to access the same memory without providing proper access synchronization.

> **Note**: TSan is only supported when running on the simulator.

While there are a few other sanitizers available — such as the **Address Sanitizer** or the **Main Thread Checker** — the only one you'll need to actively use at this point is the **Thread Sanitizer**. The other sanitizers are either meant for other languages, or are on by default.

Getting Started

Open up the Xcode project provided in this chapter's **starter** folder. It's a pretty simple-looking app that writes to a variable in two separate locations. Build and run the app; you won't see any issues. If you look at the code of **MainViewController.swift**, though, you can see you're clearly utilizing the `counter` property in different dispatch queues.

Is there any issue with your code? Probably! But you can easily catch and confirm this and other threading issues with the Thread Sanitizer.

Enabling Sanitization

The first step to checking your code with the Thread Sanitizer is enabling it. Edit the scheme by pressing Command-< or by clicking on the **Concurrency** scheme next to where you select the build device, then perform these steps:

1. Select **Run**, if it's not already selected.
2. Switch to the **Diagnostics** tab.
3. Uncheck the **Address Sanitizer**.
4. Check the **Thread Sanitizer**.

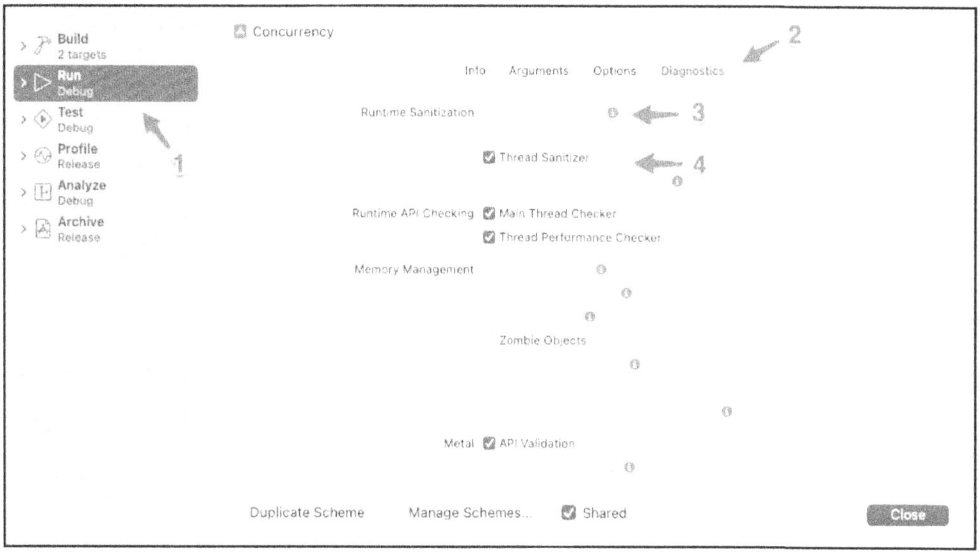

The **Address Sanitizer** and the **Thread Sanitizer** can't both be selected at the same time.

Once you've enabled the thread sanitizer, close the dialog window. Then, head over to **ContentView.swift**, comment out the call to `Thread.sleep(forTimeInterval:)` and then build and run your app.

Almost immediately, you'll notice that Xcode emits a threading issue, and you're shown that you have an access race in your closure.

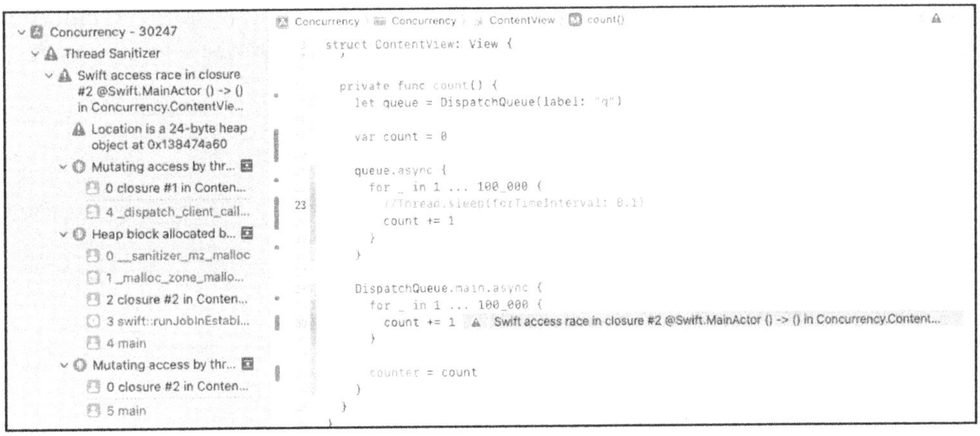

Switch to the **Issue Navigator** (Command-5). If you expand the stack trace show you'll see exactly where Xcode found the issues. You can click on the lines to be taken to that point in your source code.

It's Not Code Analysis

It's important to keep in mind that the Thread Sanitizer is **runtime** analysis. What that means is that, if an issue doesn't occur during execution, it won't be flagged. If you look at the code in **ContentView**, you'll see this, around line 23:

```
Thread.sleep(forTimeInterval: 0.1)
```

Uncomment that line of code and run the app again. This time, the app runs without any issues. Why is that? Even though you accessed the `count` variable across multiple threads, those accesses didn't end up happening at the same time.

The important takeaway is that you should try to run using the Thread Sanitizer frequently — and not just once. Enabling the sanitizer has a pretty steep performance impact of anywhere between 2x to 20x CPU slowdown, and yet, you should run it often or otherwise integrate it into your workflow, so you don't miss out on all of these sneaky threading issue!

Xcode Keeps Getting Smarter

Apple continues to improve runtime analysis of your apps even without the Thread Sanitizer. You know how important it is, by now, to always execute UI tasks on the main thread. If you forget, your app will abort at runtime in debugging. In years past, you'd have had to use the Thread Sanitizer to identify such a mistake.

Xcode does such a good job of flagging errors at runtime that it was actually quite difficult to come up with an example for this chapter!

Where to Go From Here?

You've seen how important the Thread Sanitizer is to ensuring stable apps for your customers. I suggest you enable the sanitizer at the start of app development and leave it on until you find that it is impacting the performance of testing. Once it has reached an impactful point, then disable it but continue to run at regular intervals.

Apple's official documentation is always available to you at Diagnosing memory, thread, and crash issues early (https://developer.apple.com/documentation/xcode/diagnosing-memory-thread-and-crash-issues-early). You might also look into the various continuous integration techniques available. Many of them will allow the Thread Sanitizer to be utilized during automated testing.

13 Conclusion

Congratulations! You've just completed your first step into concurrency mastery.

The skills and knowledge you've gained throughout this book are bound to serve you for many years to come. Where others might get flustered trying to resolve performance issues or trying to understand how the third-party libraries they use work, you now possess in-depth knowledge of how these lower concurrency levels work in Cocoa development, and iOS development specifically.

We hope you've enjoyed this book and can already see yourself putting your newly found knowledge into good use. Also, don't forget you can always pick this book up as a great reference to Grand Central Dispatch, Operations, or any other concurrency-related topic, when needed.

If you're more of a visual learner, much of this book's content is available in our "iOS Concurrency with GCD and Operations" video course:

- https://www.kodeco.com/9461083-ios-concurrency-with-gcd-and-operations

If you have any questions or comments as you work through this book, please stop by our forums at https://forums.kodeco.com and look for the particular forum category for this book.

Thank you again for purchasing this book. Your continued support is what makes the tutorials, books, videos, conferences and other things we do at Kodeco possible, and we truly appreciate it!

Wishing you *concurrent* success in everything you do,

– The *Concurrency by Tutorials* team

Made in the USA
Monee, IL
06 April 2026

47799492R00070